From Sorrow To Amazing Grace
One Cop's Journey

Keith Knotek

Burning Bulb
PUBLISHING

From Sorrow to Amazing Grace: One Cop's Journey
By Keith Knotek

ISBN: 978-1-948278-50-8 (Paperback)

Now for the legal disclaimer:

Burning Bulb Publishing
P.O. Box 4721
Bridgeport, WV 26330-4721
United States of America
www.BurningBulbPublishing.com

Tears of a Cop

* Author Unknown

I have been where you fear to be.
I have seen what you fear to see.
I have done what you fear to do.
All these things I've done for you.
I am the one you lean upon.
The one you cast your scorn upon.
The one you bring your troubles to,
All these people I've been to you.
The one you ask to stand apart.
The one you feel should have no heart.
The one you call the officer in blue.
But I am human, just like you.
And through the years I've come to see
That I am not what you ask of me.
So take this badge and take this gun.
Will you take it?
Will anyone?
And when you watch a person die,
And hear a battered baby cry.
Then so you think that you can be
All those things you ask of me?

Contents

Statements of Support for
From Sorrow to Amazing Grace-
One Cop's Journey

Readers' Favorite ® announces the review of the Christian - Non-Fiction book "From Sorrow to Amazing Grace" by Keith Knotek.

Readers' Favorite is one of the largest book review and award contest sites on the Internet. They have earned the respect of renowned publishers like Random House, Simon & Schuster, and Harper Collins, and have received the "Best Websites for Authors" and "Honoring Excellence" awards from the Association of Independent Authors.

From Sorrow to Amazing Grace: One Cop's Journey by Keith R. Knotek is the author's story of being an alcoholic in recovery, husband, father, son, friend, child of God, and a retired police officer. The memoir gives glimpses of his life which have been a series of ups and downs, and how the emotional scars inflicted upon him went unchecked and unaddressed for a long time. His story is that of pride, selfishness, brokenness, forgiveness, redemption, hope, faith, belief, strength, perseverance, and redemption through Jesus Christ. This memoir is all about hope and giving readers the confidence and courage to face their future, and his words show how with God's support everything is possible.

From Sorrow to Amazing Grace is honest and straightforward. He throws light on living in a safe environment growing up and how he was keen to be in law enforcement. He captures his struggles, stress, and his PTSD, and what is admirable is the way he overcame his struggles and difficulties by putting complete faith in Jesus Christ. I enjoyed reading this book and the author's honesty. It takes a lot of strength to come out in the open and speak about one's alcoholism, alcohol-induced escapades, and PTSD, and many readers undergoing similar challenges will easily relate to his words. This book is a good way to understand the life of a police officer and healing through Jesus Christ."

- **MAMTA MADHAVEN**
For Readers' Favorite ®

Nonfiction Author Book Awards

From Sorrow to Amazing Grace is a non-fiction, autobiographical memoir about life before, during, and after a 30-year career in law enforcement. It is a self-help resource about battling PTSD, alcoholism, depression, and trauma through surrendering to Christ and implementing a holistic approach to resilience. Finding peace, serenity, and a daily spiritual connection with God is at the forefront of this text.

- **CHELA HARDY**
Nonfiction Authors Association

Keith neither wanted the challenge of rising from a lifetime low point, nor asked for this opportunity to serve as an example of defeat and victory for others. Nonetheless, he relates this fate of his and welcomes us readers to join him in Christian inclusivity. You will note that, in times of achievements and setbacks both, Keith's path has been that of public service. Even when things didn't go well in his life, the constant backdrop was that he was serving and protecting the rest of us. Where service can be performed, there Keith has been. This can be good enough in a lifetime, but Keith, fighting the hazards such as alcoholism and painful memories that can bedevil life, wants more. Keith's approach, which he seeks to share, is to serve and live, but in community with God and not outside of it. I bid you to read his invitation, as assuredly heartfelt and personal as if it arrived in your mail.

- DR. DAVID M. ALEGRE, LTC, USA (ret.)
Faculty Lead, Organizational Leadership Postgraduate Programs

This is a story of a valiant police officer's journey through life- his career, personal reflection, and salvation from the darkness. From Sorrow to Amazing Grace will open your eyes to the reality, the excitement, and the hardships of a life dedicated to protecting and serving. Author Keith Knotek blesses the reader through his powerful testimony and the grace by which he was saved from the darkness that so many men and women in law enforcement carry with them every day.

- JONATHAN E. HICKORY
Veteran police officer, chaplain, speaker, and author of *Break Every Chain*

Carefully detailed within this book, Keith paints a candid picture of so many other law enforcement lives around the country--broken and without hope. How comforting to know that God is the answer and healing can be found.

- KRISTI NEACE
Founder, Badge of Hope Ministries, author of *Under Fire: Marriage Through the Eyes of a Cop's Wife*

This is an honest and personal memoir about a law enforcement officer who became broken after years of exposure to violence, death, and man's inhumane treatment of others. I found myself being drawn into the story as if I was sitting right next to the author as he took to the streets on patrol. Finding salvation, redemption, and peace is not always easy after these types of experiences. However, there is a real solution, even in the darkest of situations.

- **JEFF WILLIAMS**
Pastor, The Rock Bible Fellowship,
Huntington Beach, California

Acknowledgments

I would be remiss if I did not first acknowledge our Lord and Savior, Jesus Christ, who saved us by His grace and mercy and taught the world how to love unconditionally.

To my mother, who gave me the gift of life, taught me to love, and lived as a fine example of womanhood after overcoming the hurts and trials of your childhood. We who knew you here on Earth were blessed to have had you in our lives. You are loved and missed!

To my dad, who showed me what it means to be a father. You taught me that God must come first before all other things and that everything else will fall into place as it should with God as our King. You are loved and missed! I hope that you and Mom are smiling down on us from heaven.

To my wife, Lily, and my daughters, Alexandra and Amanda, you make me want to be a better man. Even on the most challenging days of my past, you were my reason for getting out of bed and doing what needed to be done. Your unconditional love and sustained support for me is a gift. I love you all so very much, and you bless me beyond measure with the mindfulness that all good things come from the Lord!

To Jonathan Hickory, thank you for having the courage to share your personal story of your struggles as a police officer and redemption through Christ. You have been an inspiration to me in chronicling my own story.

This book is dedicated to the memory of Deputy Randal "Randy" E. Jennings (January 22, 1959 – May 21, 1997), who lived honorably and died heroically while selflessly serving the citizens of Butte County, California.

Preface

It has been over two years since the First Edition of *From Sorrow to Amazing Grace* was released. A lot has happened since that time, and I felt it was necessary to do a rewrite of the book to add content. There were actual events I remembered after the first book was released that I believe should have been included in the First Edition – so this is my opportunity to do so. I felt it was important to share with you, the reader, the additional things I have learned along my journey to finding resilience and living a blessed life with purpose and determination.

Every one of us is unique, and we all have different experiences. Some of our experiences are collectively interwoven and are easily relatable, while others are not. We have all made mistakes, been selfish, and fallen short of the glory of God – I know I have! So, I would ask for your grace as you read this book; know that God is a father of mercy and second chances. I have learned this concept the hard way, but sometimes it just takes what it takes to walk out on the bright side of darkness.

Perhaps you will learn some valuable life lessons along the way after reading this and won't have to make the same mistakes that I did. Please remember that *low points can become grow points*, and it's never too late to choose a different path.

Foreword

Keith Knotek's book *From Sorrow to Amazing Grace* is a powerful case study for my book *On Spiritual Combat.* These two books could have been written by the same person, and in one sense they were: that one "person" is the Holy Spirit speaking within two "sheepdogs". And Keith is indeed, a true sheepdog under the authority of the Great Shepherd.

Keith's life story is also a powerful manifestation of one of the lessons that I love to teach: sometimes the greatest love is not to sacrifice your life, but to live a life of sacrifice. Through turmoil and tribulation, knocked down and back up again, working with different agencies, but always for the same Master (the Great Shepherd), Keith led a life of sacrifice. He stayed on the path of a sheepdog who is called to protect the flock.

Perseverance, determination, grit, whatever you want to call it, Keith Knotek has demonstrated it in his life. And it often is one of God's greatest gifts.

In the end, broken and driven to his knees by a lifetime in the mean streets, seeing daily the darkness that most people will never know; in the end it was God, and His Amazing Grace, only God could lead Keith from defeat into victory. God's Holy Word tells us the only true path to victory: "Not by might nor by power, but by my Spirit." (Zech. 4:6)

All around us every day, an unseen combat rages. It is invisible, yet we feel it in every aspect of our lives. It is a spiritual war. It is *a battle for our souls*, and a desperate struggle for the survival of everything we love, from our children to our nation to our very civilization.

You cannot avoid this battle. You are in this spiritual combat whether or not you want it, because the enemy *will* most definitely come for you and yours. There is no escaping this enemy. There is only victory or death-salvation or damnation.

Our enemy is evil. Indeed, our enemy is the very definition of the foulest conceivable evil, and this demonic foe never stops hurting, fighting, deceiving, cheating, and killing in an endless effort to destroy all that is dear to us.

Our enemy murders, physically and spiritually. He wishes to deprive us of our lives here on earth and (far worse) eternally in heaven. Our evil, eternal foe desires to widow our spouses, orphan our children, and to fill our lives with sin, death, and despair. Our hearts, our homes, our families, our nation, our entire civilization are at stake.

Ah, but fear not! Rejoice! For however evil and powerful our enemy may be, on our side is a force of sacrificial love that is far greater than any other force in the universe. Our Supreme Commander in this war is the one who created the universe. And he loves us.

Do you believe there is evil in this world? How can anyone deny it? Then you must believe there is also a powerful force for good at work in our lives. Isn't it odd how some people can accept the presence of evil in this world, but they cannot accept God and his heavenly forces of good?

The defining challenge of the years to come is to protect our loved ones, our students, our customers, our employees, our civilization, and our very way of life from violence in the same way that we protect them from fire.

But wait. The sky is not falling. It is within our ability to meet this challenge. Through God, his Holy Spirit, and his divine Word, we will rise to the challenge, both spiritually and physically, and He will guide us on virtuous paths to defend our civilization in these dark hours.

And a loving God raises up and empowers sheepdogs like Keith Knotek to protect His flock.

J. R. R. Tolkien was a contemporary of C. S. Lewis. Lewis wrote his series *The Chronicles of Narnia* as a Christian allegory from a Protestant perspective. Tolkien's classic warrior epic, *The Lord of the Rings* was also written as a Christian allegory, but from a Catholic perspective.

In Tolkien's book, we find these classic words of hope in the darkest hour:

- All that is gold does not glitter,
- Not all those who wander are lost.
- The old that is strong does not wither,
- Deep roots are not touched by the frost.

Now, in this dark hour, let us tap the strength that is drawn from our deep Christian warrior roots, roots that have indeed endured the bitter frost. Let us seek out the strong Godly guidance that will never wither. Let us embrace the old ways, the ways of the virtuous Christian warrior, to answer the challenge of the age with the power of God's word.

And so, read Keith Knotek's book. Learn the lesson God has taught to him. Learn and apply the lesson that Keith now shares with us.

Proclaim it now throughout the land: I am a sheepdog under the authority of the Great Shepherd! He that is in me is far greater than he that is in the world! I am a child of the one true King! Endowed by my Creator with unalienable rights, empowered by my Constitution as a free citizen, inspired by my forefathers to fight for this land I love. I am a sheepdog under the authority of the Great Shepherd, and this is as far as the minions of hell are going!

- **LT. COLONEL DAVE GROSSMAN, USA (ret.)**
Author of *On Spiritual Combat, On Killing, On Combat, and Assassination Generation*

LTC David Grossman

Lt. Col. David Grossman
Biography

Lt. Col. Dave Grossman is a former West Point psychology professor, Professor of Military Science, and an Army Ranger who is the author of *On Killing, On Combat,* and *Assassination Generation.* Col. Grossman's work has been translated into many languages, and his books are required or recommended reading in colleges, military academies, and police academies around the world, to include the US Marine Corps Commandant's reading list and the FBI Academy reading list. His research was cited by the President of the United States in a national address after the Littleton, Colorado school massacre, and he has testified before the US Senate, the US Congress, and numerous state legislatures. He has served as an expert witness and consultant in state and Federal courts, to include UNITED STATES vs. TIMOTHY MCVEIGH.

He helped train mental health professionals after the Jonesboro school massacre, and he was also involved in counseling or court cases in the aftermath of the Paducah, Springfield, and Littleton school shootings. He has been called upon to write the entry on "Aggression and Violence" in the *Oxford Companion to American Military History,* three entries in the *Academic Press Encyclopedia of Violence, Peace and Conflict* and has presented papers before the national conventions of the American Medical Association, the American Psychiatric Association, the American Psychological Association, and the American Academy of Pediatrics.

He also has published several novels, and he has five US patents to his name. He has a black belt in Hojutsu, the martial art of the firearm, and has been inducted into the USA Martial Arts Hall of Fame.

Today he is the director of the Killology Research Group (www.killology.com), and since his retirement from the US Army in 1998, for over 20 years, he has been on the road between 200-300 days a year, training elite military and law enforcement organizations worldwide about the reality of combat, and he has written extensively on the current threat situation, with articles published in the Harvard Journal of Law and Public Policy and many leading law enforcement journals.

Introduction

Crash and Burn

It is May 3, 2019, and I have recently lost my friend and mentor, Dan, to a massive heart attack. I am thinking about Dan as I am driving home to Prescott Valley, Arizona, after visiting my daughters who live in Northern Nevada. The loss of Dan weighs heavily on my mind. There is a half drank bottle of whiskey on my passenger seat, and I am speeding in the middle of the Nevada desert in an effort to get home quicker. I have no knowledge that I am weaving all over the road. As I enter a small town where the speed limit drops down to 25 mph, it is too late to react to the brake lights in front of me as the lead car slows down for the posted stop sign. As I slam on the breaks, my car is sent sliding into the back of the vehicle in front of me.

Three people are injured and sent to the hospital as I am placed in handcuffs and transported to jail for driving under the influence. This nightmare couldn't be happening. After all, I was a police officer at one time! As I spent four days in jail before being released, my heart and mind turned to God. *Is this my rock bottom?* I wonder. I cry out to God to heal the injured people and to help me deal with the aftermath of what I had done. I came to realize that I had become a horrible, deceitful, prideful, selfish, and reckless person. I finally fall on my knees and ask the God of Abraham to take away my pride, self-absorption, and propensity to turn to alcohol when I am depressed.

~

My name is Keith, and I'm an alcoholic in recovery and haven't touched an alcoholic beverage in over three years. I am also a husband, father, son, friend, child of God, and a retired police officer. I am not famous. You have probably never even heard of me unless you know me personally. My life has been a series of peaks and valleys - with mountaintop highs and the lowest of lows. I had what I felt to be an exciting and rewarding career in law enforcement. But unfortunately, my experiences after thirty years in the profession left me with emotional scars that went unaddressed and unchecked until later in life.

To quote pastor and author Brennan Manning, "I am a 'ragamuffin.'" You may ask yourself, what is a ragamuffin? The term itself was coined to describe broken people, who are ragged, disreputable sinners. Ragamuffins are aware of their brokenness but are even more conscious of God's grace, mercy, and unfathomable love in their lives. My greatest awareness of myself is that Jesus Christ profoundly loves me, and I have done nothing to earn it or deserve it. Christianity is not primarily a moral code but a grace-laden mystery, thank God!

This chronicle is my true story. It is about post-traumatic stress (PST) and alcoholism while working in the public safety profession. It is a journey about a man and his pride, selfishness, brokenness, forgiveness, redemption, and sanctification through Christ Jesus. It is a testament to hope and strength. This writing is a labor of love for those currently or formerly working as professional first responders in the emergency services field and current or former military members. I am usually a very private person by nature. There was a time when I would not ever want to air my struggles in public or become vulnerable in any way whatsoever. But I feel I need to tell my story if I can help just one person. This book touches on a few of the critical incidents I've been involved with and how they negatively affected me. It is not an all-encompassing account of my entire career but a retelling of a few of my memoirs. I used to be a cynical, selfish, and broken person. However, I was able to finally overcome the trauma of the past with God's help.

I earnestly hope this book will be inspiring to you and give you the courage to face the future. Pursuing help is an act of courage in itself. We work in a critical profession where a person's actions are ridiculed just as often as driving a car or getting out of bed in the morning. It takes more fortitude to seek support and assistance than it does to drown at the bottom of a bottle or other self-destructive behaviors.

Although this is my story, I do not want to draw attention to myself or be the center of focus. The words in this book are my personal experiences, but my desire is that this reading shines a light on the very God who made the light - our loving heavenly Father. I have done nothing extraordinary, and everything good in my life has come from God. He is the reason I am still alive today and can tell my story of faith, joy, hope, and redemption. With God, all things are possible.

We live in a beautiful world that can sometimes be a vicious and dark place. May God bless and protect each one of you as you fight the good fight!

"Blessed are the peacemakers,
for they will be called children of God."
(Matthew 5:9)

Chapter 1

The Early Years

I'm no expert, but I suppose that every autobiographic story should start out with something to the effect of I was born in San Bernardino, California, in January of 1965. Lyndon Baines Johnson was still president of the United States, and the "space race" was in full swing. The Gulf of Tonkin incident, where a U.S. Navy destroyer was pursued by three north-Vietnamese navy torpedo boats, had occurred about six months prior to my birth. The Vietnam War really began to escalate at that time. On March 8, 1965, the first US combat forces arrived in Vietnam on the beaches of Da Nang. My Fair Lady won the Academy Award for Best Picture, and "Astroturf" was invented that year.

Also, that same year, The Beatles' '65 album went number one and stayed there for nine weeks. On February 1, 1965, Dr. Martin Luther King Jr. and seven hundred civil rights demonstrators were arrested in Selma, Alabama, and the red maple leaf flag became the official flag of Canada. The Los Angeles Dodgers won the 62nd World Series against the Minnesota Twins. Finally, on December 4, 1965, Gemini 7 launched with Frank Borman and Jim Lovell on board. The astronauts spent fourteen days in space and made 206 orbits around the Earth. But man had not yet walked on the moon.

There were no cellphones, laptops, voicemail, bottled water, or "cryptocurrency when I arrived on this planet." Even when it came to television, most programs were broadcast in black & white. Police officers in the United States typically carried .38 caliber revolvers with a four to six-inch barrel and earned an average of $312 per month. Officers did not carry expandable batons, Tasers, or even self-contained pepper spray canisters at that time because they had not yet been invented. Police officers did not wear beards in uniform either, as they typically had a clean-shaven, military appearance. If you think about it, 1965 was only twenty years after the end of World War II.

My father, James, was a fourth-generation American. He grew up in Milwaukee, Wisconsin, in the 30s and 40s before moving to Los Angeles in 1947. His ancestors were primarily of Prussian descent, which today would be considered portions of modern-day Germany, Austria, and Czechoslovakia. My dad's second great grandfather, August Koepke, an immigrant from Austria, fought for the Union Army in the U.S. Civil War. He was in the 26th Wisconsin Infantry, which fought in the Fredericksburg Campaign, Mud Run Campaign, and the Battle of Gettysburg. Dad graduated from Alexander Hamilton High School, Los Angeles, in 1949. He got called up for the draft to enter the Korean War but was deemed to be Category "4-F" due to his flat feet, which was a disqualifier for military service in those days. He later attended Pacific Union College in Angwin, California, and graduated with a bachelor of arts in 1963. He was accepted into graduate school at Andrews University in Berrien Springs, Michigan, where he graduated with a master of arts in theology in 1964.

Finally, in 1966, when I was a year old, my dad entered Concordia Theological Seminary on a partial scholarship. It was located in Springfield, Illinois, at that time. He worked as a substitute teacher to keep food on the table for our family. Dad graduated in 1968 with a Master of Divinity Degree and was ordained a minister in the Lutheran Church – Missouri Synod. It's needless to say I grew up in the Lutheran Church. Dad was very much the conservative hardliner and had strong opinions about how things should be. Yet, my father's view of life was somewhat naïve regarding harsh worldly matters. He wrote music, sold real estate, did odd jobs, and was part owner of a granite processing company that sold granite as landscaping material before entering the Christian ministry. Nonetheless, I loved and admired my dad, who stood five feet five inches tall in his prime.

My mother, Ruth, was a 9th-generation American, and her early ancestors hailed from England and Scotland. Her lineage traces back to King James VI of Scotland, who later became King James I of England, Scotland, and Ireland. There were also several patriots on my mother's side who fought against British rule in the American Revolutionary War. In addition, I had two third great grandfathers who fought for the North in the Union Army on both my maternal and paternal sides. Mom was born and raised in Providence, Rhode Island, before moving to Los Angeles in 1949. She and my dad married in October 1949. They were both 18 years old at the time. My mom had a rough childhood and lived with several foster families while growing up. But she overcame her difficulties and later reconciled with her mother, my Grandma Mary. Mom had a heart of gold, and people were naturally drawn to her bubbly, witty personality. She was a stay-at-home mother for most of my childhood but received her diploma and certification as a Licensed Vocational Nurse later in life.

My sister Cynthia (Cindy) was almost nine years older than me and was born in 1956. She loved the music of Aerosmith, Led Zeppelin, Rod Stewart, The Who, and Queen. Cindy was a '70s girl who wore tie-dye tops and bell-bottom jeans. She drove a souped-up '69 Oldsmobile Cutlass 442. It was painted dark metallic blue, and many young men would turn their heads and gawk as Cindy drove down the road. I attended the same high school as Cindy – eight years later, her teachers still remembered her.

After my father graduated from the seminary, his first assignment was a "dual parish" in Kern County, California. In other words, he was the pastor of two different churches that were located 50 miles apart from each other; one in North Edwards and the other in Tehachapi. Our family lived in North Edwards because that church provided a parsonage - church-provided housing for our family. Dad would do Sunday morning services for the North Edwards congregation, and then he'd make the 50-mile trek up the mountain to Tehachapi and would conduct the church service for that congregation. Since North Edwards is located next to Edwards Air Force Base, my parents got to know many military families. Many airmen were parishioners at the North Edwards congregation. In addition, Edwards Air Force Base was instrumental in the experimental and testing phase during the Space Race.

Several Air Force church members tried to encourage my dad to become an Air Force chaplain. My dad had all the qualifications and had not yet reached his fortieth birthday. He was an ordained Lutheran minister and had a Master of Divinity degree. He could have gone into the U.S. Air Force as a captain with his credentials as all service branches were short on chaplains at that time. However, the Vietnam War was in full swing, and my dad probably would have been deployed overseas. He felt that being a father to his young children and serving locally was his calling rather than going into the military.

One of the congregants from our church, Major Charles "Chuck" R. Rosburg, was an Air Force test pilot. He flew U-2 spy planes, among other aircraft. On the day that our family was moving into the parsonage, a U-2 made a low pass over our house, and it rocked its wings back and forth. That was Major Rosburg's way of welcoming us to the neighborhood. He later gave my dad and me a tour of a couple of hangars on base. One of the structures contained an X-15 rocket plane, and I was able to walk underneath the aircraft and touch it. I was standing underneath a piece of history and didn't even know it at that time.

On January 27, 1969, while participating in an air force exchange program, Major Rosburg was killed while testing a Hawker Siddeley Harrier Jump Jet in Dunsfold, Surrey, Great Britain, as part of a U.S. air force/Royal air force exchange program. Later, lateral control was lost following a vertical take-off and while in an accelerating transition. As a result, the aircraft side-slipped and struck the ground with 90 degrees of bank. Major Rosburg ejected sideways from the cockpit and was struck by part of the aircraft's canopy. His was a significant loss to the North Edward's community. As a side note, I should mention that five months after the death of Major Rosburg, the Apollo 11 spacecraft was launched, and Neil Armstrong became the first man to walk on the moon.

North Edwards, population one thousand, had only one small grocery store called Kelley's Market and not a whole lot of anything else. I attended Richard B. Lynch Elementary School (now closed) during my kindergarten year. When my parents wanted to do their major grocery shopping, they'd drive into Lancaster, which had a resident population of around thirty thousand at the time. There was another small town located next to Lancaster called Rosamond. The great thing about Rosamond was its drive-in movie theatre at the time. My parents would dress me in my pajamas, and we'd go watch movies there from time to time during the evening hours.

In 1971, my dad took a new church assignment at Faith Lutheran Church located in Capistrano Beach, California. In 1989, "Capo Beach" was annexed into the City of Dana Point. I attended Palisades Elementary School for my first through third-grade years. At that time, El Toro Marine Corps Air Station was an active duty air station in the 70s, and I used to watch all kinds of military aircraft fly over our house. When the jet engines would rumble our neighborhood, my dad used to say, "Ah, that's the sound of freedom, son!" This was around the time when I started learning the importance of family, faith, patriotism, and tradition. Oh, how I miss those simple days.

I have fond memories of my childhood, like bobbing for apples around Halloween time and singing, or at least trying to sing, Christmas carols during the Christmas season. I remember decorating our fake white-colored, plastic Christmas tree with the large old school lights and strands of tinsel. It gave me a warm and fuzzy, happy feeling inside when our tree was on display. My dad usually read me bedtime stories and then had me do the reading as I got older and improved my reading ability. We didn't live in a castle, nor did my parents drive fancy cars. But I felt rich in love, and all of my physical needs were met.

I loved airplanes, anything having to do with astronauts or going to the moon, and policemen. I remember being around six years old when a couple of sheriff's deputies were on their meal break. As my parents and I were leaving the restaurant, I stopped at their table and started asking them questions like, "What's all of that stuff on your belt?" One of the deputies was very friendly, and he showed me the cases and pouches he had for his keys, handcuffs, extra ammo, and such. In retrospect, they were probably annoyed that a curious little kid had interrupted their dinner break. But nonetheless, they were good about the whole thing.

My dad taught me to pray every night before bed and at mealtime. I routinely witnessed Mom and Dad praying together and being happy and joyful in the Lord. My parents used to talk about miracles that happened in their lives and the power, love, and awesomeness of God. I certainly believed in God and His Son, Jesus, but I knew nothing of the Holy Spirit. I didn't know how to receive the gift of the Holy Spirit, nor did I live a godly life. As I grew up, the spiritual component of my upbringing went by the wayside. I tried to do what was morally right but did not seek God's will. I went to church as an adult because that was just something I was supposed to do.

One vivid memory I have of my Capistrano Beach years was of a family that lived in our neighborhood. You see, we lived in a predominantly white, middle-class neighborhood, but an African-American family lived a few houses down from us. The father was a U.S. Secret Service agent, and he and his wife had several younger children. This was during the Nixon era, and the "Western White House," as it was known, was in the next town over – San Clemente.

One day when I was around six years old, I waved to my dad as he was headed back to work after taking his lunch break at our home. There was a group of neighborhood kids in the middle of the street. They were on bicycles and circled around the little African American boy that lived on the block. They were shouting the "N-word" at him. I watched my father stop and exit his car. He yelled at the kids, and they all scattered. I don't know what he said to them, but I'm sure it wasn't very pleasant. When my dad returned home at the end of the day, I asked him what that word meant, as I had never heard it before. He told me that it was a "derogative word that some people use for black people." I'll never forget that. I was just a little boy myself and was sheltered from such bad behavior. But my dad did the right thing and came to the little boy's defense. I'd like to think that times have changed for the better since those days.

The Capistrano Beach assignment lasted about three years. Then my dad took a new position at Redeemer Lutheran Church located in Huntington Beach, California. The family moved there in 1974. Some of my fondest memories as a youngster are of growing up in Huntington Beach, which was also known as "Surf City USA." The city had much to offer like beaches, surfing, a moderate climate, plenty of shopping, a large community college, many parks, and a variety of different housing options.

My greatest formative years were spent in Huntington Beach. I moved to that community as a child, and by the time I moved away, I was a young man working in a career field. It was a great place to learn about life's lessons and to grow up. Looking back on my time there, I became aware that I was truly blessed and still am today.

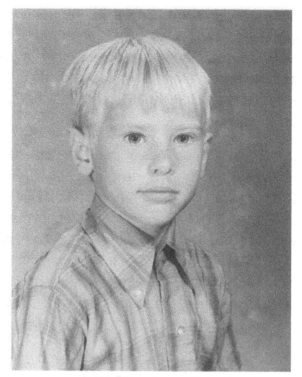

Keith, at age 8

Chapter 2

The Huntington Beach Years

I attended Spring View School, which was a K-8 school at the time. Spring View eventually became a middle school with the population growth of Huntington Beach. My dad usually dropped me off at school in the morning on his way to work. I'd walk home at the end of the school day. On my walks home from school, I'd have to cross a busy street called Heil Avenue. Students were assisted across the heavily traveled road by a crossing guard. I remember how fascinated I was by the appearance of the crossing guard. Although I knew he wasn't a police officer, he kind of looked like one. He wore a khaki-colored uniform, orange vest, and a white police-style hat. He used a police department issued whistle to get drivers' attention. I recall him being an amiable fellow, and thus he was a good ambassador for his employer, the Huntington Beach Police Department.

On days when I had no homework or at least pretended not to have homework, my friends and I would ride our bicycles everywhere. We'd ride all around the neighborhood or to Chris Carr Park, where there was a good size pond. We'd catch pollywogs and bluegill in that pond. Sometimes we'd bring scraps of bread to feed the ducks. Sometimes we'd go for a long bike ride to Old World German Village, which was a little replica 17th century, German-style shopping area. There was an excellent candy store there where my friends and I would spend our pocket change if we had any.

Sundays were always church days. My dad would do two-morning services for the growing congregation. I attended Sunday school in the early morning and then the later church service after the conclusion of Sunday school. After the whole church experience was over for the day, the family would typically go out to lunch with one or more of the congregants. I remember always looking forward to Sunday evenings because that was when the TV programs Lassie, Mutual of Omaha's Wild Kingdom, and Wonderful World of Disney were on.

It was December 1975 and the end of the Vietnam War. I was ten years old and had volunteered to be in our church's Christmas play. I was to take on the role of King Herod. One day I walked to church to practice for the upcoming play. I read my lines, and after practice, I started walking home, which was about two miles from the church. As I approached the intersection of Heil Avenue and Springdale Avenue, I waited for my light to turn green before entering the crosswalk. As I stepped onto the street, a small Datsun pickup truck was approaching me at a high rate of speed. Within a second, I looked at the driver, who was looking to his left. I could clearly see he had no idea what was going on ahead of him or that I was directly in front of his vehicle. As I tried to take evasive action, bang – lights out! The truck struck me and dragged me a short distance around the corner before coming to a stop.

As I started to regain consciousness, I could feel that I had the wind knocked out of me upon impact. I remember a gas station attendant from the Shell Station on the corner pulling me out from underneath the pickup truck. There was a fire station next to the gas station, so firefighter-paramedics were on the scene within a minute or two. The medics checked me out, and an ambulance crew and police unit also responded. Lo and behold, I hadn't a scratch on me. I had no scratches, no abrasions, and no broken bones.

My dad was notified of the accident at the church, and he responded to the scene immediately. He asked me if I was alright, and I said, "I think so." The first responders said there didn't appear to be anything else for them to do for me. These days they would have tried to talk my father into making me take an ambulance ride to the hospital. My father subsequently drove me home, and we told my mom what had happened. I was wearing a button-down shirt with a T-shirt underneath. My mom noticed one of the top buttons had been torn off during the accident, and part of my undershirt was exposed. She then pointed out the fact that there was a tire tread track mark going across the T-shirt. The truck had actually run me over with its right front tire. This was nothing short of a miracle – praise be to God! I believed that I was saved through divine intervention. But as a young kid, I believed in God and yet had no real relationship with Him. I didn't have the spiritual or emotional maturity to know how to have a spiritual connection with God.

It was 1976 and our nation's bicentennial. I thought I wanted to be a minister like my father until I discovered the television show "Adam-12," which was about the adventures of two Los Angeles Police patrol officers, Pete Malloy and Jim Reed. Although I didn't know it at the time, the technical advisors for the TV program were actually currently working LAPD officers. The show was a relatively realistic representation of law enforcement and how its officers operated at that time. I was fascinated by law enforcement and everything that had to do with policing. The profession sparked my curiosity and my interest so much so that my dad built me a mock police station out of plywood in our backyard so I could adequately play "cops and robbers" with my friends. I was also allowed to watch such television shows as Police Story and The Rookies.

I was young, naïve, and hadn't a care in the world. I lived in a safe and comfortable environment. I ate, slept, played, went to school, went to church, watched television, and figured that someday I'd marry and start a family. I paid no attention to what I was going to become when I reached adulthood but instead just focused on the here and now. I thought I had unlimited time to figure out what type of post-secondary education and career I would have in the future. But the future eventually came to me as time waits for no man.

Chapter 3

The Police Explorer Years

I graduated 8th grade in the spring of 1979 and returned to school that fall as a freshman at Marina High School. I remember being petrified to go to a "big kid school" on a new campus. At that time, the student population at MHS was around 3,000. There were many students who had attended other middle schools the previous school year. So it's needless to say there were a lot of kids at MHS that I didn't know. It was awkward that freshman year. But by the time my sophomore year rolled around, I had joined the track team, school newspaper, and the German club. I started making new friends and kind of enjoyed being at a new school.

When I was 15 years old, I finally told my parents I wanted to become a police officer instead of a pastor. My mom told me she supported me and thought I'd be a good cop when I got older. My dad, however, was disappointed and said to me that law enforcement is too dangerous. He went on to say that he would worry about me all of the time if I became a police officer. It's kind of funny considering that it's usually the moms who worry about such things. My father's concerns went in one ear and out of the other. This was it, I reluctantly broke the news to my parents, and a great weight had been lifted from my shoulders. I could finally pursue what I really wanted to do. There was no stopping me!

I turned 16 years old in 1981 and decided I should probably do something that would prepare me for a career in law enforcement. I heard about the police explorer post that the Huntington Beach Police Department sponsored. It was a youth program for high school students that had an interest in the law enforcement profession. I called the front desk officer at the police department, and he gave me some information about the explorers. He told me that meeting nights were on Thursday evenings which worked out perfectly for me. I had recently obtained my driver's license, and nobody needed to use the family car on Thursday nights!

In the early 80s, Huntington Beach PD was the premier police agency in Orange County, CA. It had around 180 sworn police officers at that time and was one of the highest-paid law enforcement agencies in Southern California. They had cutting-edge technology and some of the best equipment for the time period. The city was 32.1 square miles and had a growing population of about 165,000 back then. The department was known for hiring lateral police officers from agencies in Los Angeles County and had an aggressive enforcement stance.

I finally attended my first police explorer meeting in November 1981. Prior to the start, I watched the whole group of police explorers, ranging in age from 15 to 19 years old, getting inspected in an enclosed patio-type area. There were probably 20 teenagers dressed in uniforms, and the senior-most explorers, along with several police officers, were walking up and down through the assembly of explorers who were standing information and at the position of attention. Some of the kids got dropped to do pushups for minor uniform infractions, among other trivial violations.

The explorers filed into a large conference room for training after the conclusion of the inspection. I remember the training topic was on California Penal Code section 459 – burglary. The officer presenting the class talked about the corpus delicti of the crime and what elements were necessary to constitute the crime of vehicle, residential, and commercial burglary. I thought to myself, "Wow, this looks really interesting. I think I can do this and be good at it!"

At the end of the meeting, one of the police officers, Bill White, introduced himself to me, as did the explorer captain. I later found out that Bill White was a retired major who served in the United States Marine Corps. He was a longtime reserve officer for the police department. He provided me with an application and told me to come to the next meeting if I was still interested in becoming an explorer. Officer White told me to wear "appropriate" attire and to be prepared to go through an oral board. Since I had no idea what an oral board was, I had to clarify that it was like a job interview with a panel of interviewers.

I showed up at the police station the following Thursday evening with my application in hand. I was escorted into the department's library, where Officer White and two senior explorers were waiting for me. They asked me a series of questions like, "Why do you want to join the police explorers," and "Have you used drugs of any kind, etc.?" After the inquisition was over, they made me wait outside of the room. A few minutes later, Officer White came out and told me that I had passed my interview. I was in!

I continued to go to explorer meetings and trained on different law enforcement topics. We learned about firearms safety and got to go to the pistol range a few times. We learned about radio codes, report writing, traffic control, and other neat stuff. I started making new friends in the program, like Ed McLaughlin, George Murray, Doug Bannister, and Randy Williams. Ed and Randy were the same age as me, and George and Doug were a year younger than the rest of us. These guys ultimately became lifetime friends with whom I have stayed in touch for decades.

I also started to get to know some of the police officers, like Dan Fuson, Bert Atkins, and Carrie Drayer, who helped run the explorer program. The explorer program coordinator was a police officer named JB Hume. He was a rather large framed, stocky fellow with sandy brown hair and a typical 80s-style police mustache. He was a former explorer himself, and he had a heart of gold. He was a school resource officer when school was in session, and he worked patrol when school was out for the summer break.

Ride-a-longs were like the ultimate cool thing for an explorer to do. But explorers must have completed a four-day explorer "academy" before they were allowed to go out on patrol with an officer. I got to attend an explorer academy at Camp Pendleton. We spent long days and nights drilling and learning about different law enforcement-related subjects. We all slept in Quonset huts, and our bunks and footlockers were routinely inspected over the four-day period. I remember doing a lot of running and pushups! On February 15, 1982, our group was bussed back to Huntington Beach, where a graduation ceremony was held in the quad at Marina High School.

Finally, in March 1982, I got to go on my first ride-a-long with JB Hume on dayshift. We were assigned the "2-7 Charlie" area, which was the city's southern portion. I was a little bit nervous but excited at the same time. Prior to going 10-8 (in-service), JB took me to the secure parking lot, where all of the police vehicles were parked. He showed me how to do a patrol vehicle inspection on our 1978 Pontiac Le Mans police car, which included making sure all of the vehicle's emergency lighting equipment, siren, PA system, and electronics were working properly. We checked the trunk for road flares, a fire extinguisher, an emergency blanket, and a first-aid kit.

After making sure our patrol unit functioned properly, JB told me to tell the dispatcher that we were in service. Oh, my gosh, I've never talked on the radio before! What should I do? Should I take a breath before I talk or exhale as I'm speaking into the microphone? Oh, here it goes, "2-7 Charlie, 10-8." Wow, I did it! That wasn't too difficult. We rolled through the security gate, and JB drove us to our patrol area. I remember how uncomfortable my waist and hips felt as I sat in the passenger seat. I was wearing a Sam Browne style belt and carrying handcuffs, a portable radio, keys, a folding knife, and a heavy three-cell flashlight. That was a lot of weight to be carrying, and I wasn't used to it yet.

One of the first calls of the day was a report of a suspicious man sitting in a vehicle that was parked in a residential neighborhood. The reporting party advised that the occupied vehicle was not known to him or her and had not been seen in the neighborhood before. We responded to the area, and JB pulled in behind the car. He told me to stay in the patrol vehicle while he made contact with the driver. JB stood at the driver's side door for a couple of minutes and talked to the man seated in the driver's seat. He came back to the patrol car and ran a record check of the individual.

JB told me that the man in the car was drunk and that he was going to arrest him for being intoxicated in public. He left the patrol car again and re-contacted the driver. JB asked the man to step out of the vehicle, but the man refused. JB opened the driver's side door and again asked the man to step out, and he finally complied. When JB asked the man to turn around and place his hands behind his back, the man took an awkward swing at JB. The man ended up on the ground with JB placing him in a "carotid sleeper hold." The man passed out, and JB was able to place him in handcuffs. Holy moly, did

I just really witness a guy get "choked out?" Yes, I did, and it was real life, not something I saw on television! I wonder if I'll learn how to do that one someday?

We transported the man to jail and deposited him accordingly. Then we hit the streets again and headed back to our patrol area. JB made a few traffic stops, and he had me run the record checks so that I could get used to talking on the radio. I was really starting to get the hang of it. I recall JB making a traffic stop, and the driver had a suspended license. JB ended up impounding the vehicle, and he had me fill out the CHP Form 180 – impound sheet. I just filled in the blanks – it wasn't rocket science. After doing some traffic enforcement, we headed off for a lunch break. We both brought our lunch, so we stopped at one of the fire stations and ate. The firefighters always treated the police officers great and vice versa.

After lunch, we headed back out on patrol. As we were traveling northbound on Magnolia Street, we had to slow and come to a stop for a red signal light at Adams Avenue. As we were sitting at the intersection, I saw a Buick going westbound on Adams Avenue. The driver, who was an elderly male, pulled into the left turn lane to turn onto southbound Magnolia Street. Unfortunately, there was a young man riding a motorcycle who was traveling eastbound on Adams Avenue. I could see it coming before it happened – smash! The driver in the Buick turned left in front of the motorcyclist. The motorcycle kind of bounced off of the car as the rider flew over the hood of the Buick and landed in the middle of the intersection.

JB threw the patrol car into park and bailed out. He was running towards the injured motorcyclist. JB gave me no instructions, so I just tried to recall in my five months of police explorer experience what I should do. I grabbed the radio "mike" in the car and called it in to dispatch. I activated the unit's emergency overhead lights and popped the trunk. JB began administering first-aid to the motorcyclist, who had suffered a compound fracture on his right tibia bone, which was protruding from his right leg. I set up a flare pattern and directed traffic around the accident. Little did I know at the time that I would subsequently be subpoenaed as a witness and would have to give a deposition in the motorcyclist's civil suit against the driver of the Buick.

Wow, what a day so far! We finished out the shift going to a few more calls for service before "heading back to the barn." At the end of the day, JB told me he was impressed with the way I handled myself for only having been an explorer for a short time. I was young, naïve, impressionable, and had no real-life experience. I am almost certain that JB's compliment caused my 17-year-old head to swell. JB later wrote a letter of commendation for me, which was sent up the chain of command to the chief's office. The chief at the time, Earle Robitaille, in turn, wrote a nice commendation on my behalf based on what JB had written.

One of my next ride-a-longs was with a swing shift officer named Mike O'Riley. Officer O'Riley was a younger man, probably in his mid-20s. He fit the profile of a "surfer dude." He was buffed out, very physically fit, and was quite the ladies' man. Within the first couple of hours of the shift, we received a gunshot suicide call at an apartment complex off Beach Boulevard and Warner Avenue. We arrived on the scene and were met by the reporting party, who was waiting for us just outside the apartment. Mike and I entered the apartment, where we found a suicide note that was left on the kitchen table. We walked into the bedroom and found a woman lying on the bed. There was a single gunshot wound to her chest and a five-shot, .38 caliber revolver next to the body. Mike told me to wait outside and not to let anyone inside while he conducts his preliminary investigation.

As I waited outside and in front of the apartment, a few neighbors walked by and asked me what had happened. I don't remember specifically what I told them, but I do recall trying to ease their concerns in case they thought it was a homicide or something. As the neighbors came and went, I could clearly see a man was approaching me. He was walking fast and with a purpose. As he got closer, I could see that it was Ed, my best friend's father. I asked him, "What are you doing here?" Ed replied, "I got a phone call that my sister shot herself." My heart sank, and I was filled with sadness! My close friend's aunt had committed suicide. Mike wrapped up his investigation, and the rest of the shift was uneventful.

I continued in the explorer program for two years and made the rank of explorer sergeant. I went on a lot of ride-a-longs and began to earn the trust of some of the officers I rode with regularly. They knew that if they gave me a simple job to do, it would be completed without any issues. I rode with JB Hume a lot since he was the explorer program coordinator. I really began to develop a friendship with him, and he allowed me to do a lot of tasks that some of the other officers wouldn't think of letting me do. I was on several ride-a-longs with JB, where we were in vehicle pursuits. I saw him point guns at suspects and chase after people on foot a few times. It got my adrenaline pumping and caused me to want to become a police officer even more. It was so exciting and fast-paced at times, and I wanted to be a part of it. My explorer years sealed my decision to go into law enforcement.

Huntington Beach Police, 1978 Pontiac Le Mans

Keith, at age 16.

Chapter 4

The Cadet Years

The Huntington Beach Police Department had cadets, which was a paid position in which college students could work for the department while attending school. Cadets were allowed to work up to 24 hours a week if they carried a full-time college course load, at least 12-semester units. Cadets could work 40 hours per week during the summer break. After graduating from high school in 1983, I decided this was the path I wanted to take. I applied to be a cadet and enrolled for the fall semester at Golden West College. I chose to major in criminal justice. The PD wasn't hiring cadets at the time, so I got a part-time job as a campus security officer at the same college where I was also a student.

I took a full course load and was enjoying attending classes in which I was actually interested, whereas high school was all about taking the state's mandated courses of study and curriculum. I found that I had learned so much in the police explorer program that I was able to pull off A grades in my Police Orientation and Report Writing courses without too much effort. I ended up with a B grade in both Criminal Law and Introduction to Criminal Justice. I only wanted to take criminal justice-related classes at that time because that was what interested me at the time. I didn't think about getting any type of academic degree until later in life.

In January 1984, I received a notice in the mail to participate in a written examination and physical agility test for the position of police cadet. I was in great physical shape at the time. I was 5-9 and weighed about 145 pounds soaking wet! I had a 28-inch waist and could run laps forever. A group of about 20 of us arrived at the police station and took the written test. After we finished the written exam, we were directed to drive to the Golden West College athletic field to complete the physical agility test. It consisted of running a mile and a half; scaling a six-foot wall, scaling a six-foot chain-link fence; doing pushups, pull-ups, and sit-ups; running an obstacle course, and a simulated rescue in which we had to drag a 165-pound dummy 50 feet. I aced the test and was subsequently scheduled for an oral board the following week.

On the day of the oral board, I walked into an interview room on the second floor of the police facility. A sergeant and two officers were seated behind a table, and a single chair where I was supposed to sit was located across from them. They looked so stoic and serious! These were men that I had seen quite frequently during my tenure as an explorer. I knew that JB put a good word in for me with the oral board panelists, but that day they looked like they meant business! I sat down and tried to calm myself. They asked me their series of questions, and I had a reasonably clear answer for each query. However, I remember walking out of the police station that day, having no definitive feeling about passing the interview. I was sweating underneath the business suit I wore that day, and I couldn't wait to get home and put on a pair of shorts and a clean T-shirt.

A week or two later, I received a notice in the mail that my ranking for the cadet position was number one and to contact the personnel officer for further instructions. Yahoo, I made it! I contacted Officer Morris, the personnel officer, and made an appointment to see him. I went to his office, where he gave me a very lengthy background investigation packet to complete, and he scheduled me for a pre-employment polygraph examination.

While the background investigation got underway, I showed up for my polygraph examination. I remember being incredibly nervous as I have never had to do such a thing before. The polygraph examiner did his best to make me feel at ease, but I heard stories of people failing their polygraph even though they were telling the truth. One of the questions he asked me prior to the examination was how many alcoholic beverages do you normally consume? That was a trick question because the drinking age in California was 21 years old, and I was only 19. If I told him I don't drink alcoholic beverages, I'd be a liar. If I told him I would only have one or two beers in a party atmosphere, it would make me an underage drinker and a lawbreaker. I decided to tell the truth and went with the latter answer, at which time the polygraph examiner, who was also a police officer, said, "Well, if you're going to be one of us, you're going to have to learn to drink a lot more beer!" Oh, what a relief! Little did I know how profound that statement really was at the time.

By this time, I was in my first serious romantic relationship with a girl named Alana. She was a year younger than me, and we met in the police explorer program. Alana was a blond-haired, blue-eyed beauty with a sweet disposition. I can honestly say that I was in love for the first time. I took her to her senior prom in 1984, the year she graduated high school.

My first assignment as a cadet was not all that high speed. I was assigned to the front desk at the police station and assisted the desk officer with answering phone calls and assisting walk-ins. I also entered information into the computer-assisted dispatch system, which was cutting-edge technology for its time. But this was really the assignment where I was able to learn and perfect my report writing skills. We wrote a lot of reports at the front desk, anything from petty theft to vehicle burglaries. This was where I also learned how to dust vehicles for latent fingerprints and how to take crime scene photographs.

If it were a slow shift at the front desk, I would often go out on a ride-a-long with one of the officers. One evening when working a swing shift, one of the officers, Willie Westerfield, took me out on patrol. He was working "6-Charlie," the downtown beat. We drove out to our patrol area, and Willie decided to park the patrol unit next to El Don Liquor at 5th Street and Pacific Coast Highway (PCH). He said, "Come on, let's get out and go on foot." It was probably around 11:00 PM as we walked east along Pacific Coast Highway in front of Cagney's by the Sea Bar and Grill.

As we rounded the corner at PCH and Main Street, we saw a pickup truck parked partially on the sidewalk. There was a guy apparently passed out in the bed of the truck. Willie tried to wake him up, but the man was so drunk it took Willie to give him a sternum rub to wake him from his slumber. When the man came to, he became belligerent and uncooperative. He got out of the bed of the truck and squared off with Willie like he wanted to fight. When Willie told him to turn around and put his hands behind his back, the drunk guy clenched his fists, at which time Willie utilized a carotid sleeper hold and took him down to the ground. As this event was unfolding, I called for additional units over the radio since Willie was a little busy at the moment. Willie and I were finally able to place the man in handcuffs before a second unit arrived. So, that made the second time I saw the carotid sleeper hold being used.

My second assignment was by far the most fun of all of my cadet assignments. I was assigned to the Traffic Bureau as a parking enforcement and traffic control officer. My call sign was "53-G," and I got to go anywhere in the city that I wanted.

I took radio calls of illegally parked and abandoned vehicles in addition to responding to traffic collisions to conduct traffic control. I almost felt like I was my own boss because I was no longer tied to sitting at the front desk for a whole shift. During dayshift, I would often park in the downtown area next to the beach and conducted foot patrol looking for illegally parked vehicles. I had a lot of interaction with the public – some of it good and some of it not so great. Working and growing up in a beach city was great. It afforded me opportunities to go surfing on a regular basis.

When I was about 19 years old, I went surfing on the south side of the Huntington Beach Pier. As I was paddling out to catch a wave, I got caught in a riptide. It started to pull me further out into the ocean and carried me northward towards the pier. I tried to paddle myself in a southerly direction parallel to the beach, but the current was just too strong. The ocean swept me underneath the pier, and a wave that was starting to form slammed me against one of the pier's pylons. I pushed off of the pylon with my bare feet, and as I did, the razor-sharp barnacles that were attached to the structure cut the bottom of my feet. Somehow I managed to get out of the riptide, and I paddled to shore without any further incident. This was another time that God saw fit to keep me alive. He brought me out of danger with some lacerations to my feet. I went home, told my mother what had happened, and never surfed again.

One summer evening in 1985, my friend Ed, who was also an HBPD cadet, and I went to downtown Huntington Beach. I don't recall specifically what we were doing downtown, but we were walking on Main Street near Pacific Coast Highway. As we approached the intersection going towards the beach, I saw a small Japanese pickup truck traveling south on Pacific Coast Highway, and he wasn't slowing down for the red traffic light. As people, including Ed and me, were using the crosswalk to cross the busy intersection, the truck came barreling through and struck a female pedestrian. The female flew up in the air and landed on the asphalt as the driver of the truck kept going.

Ed and I ran to aid the seriously injured woman. I'll never forget she was wearing a blue dress that had been pulled up over her head. Ed and I pulled her dress down to give the woman some semblance of dignity. Other onlookers went inside a local business to call 911 as Ed and I tended to her badly injured body as best as we could. Emergency personnel started to arrive at the scene. An HBPD traffic officer interviewed Ed and me, at which time we provided him with a fairly accurate description of the suspect's vehicle along with a partial license plate number.

When I went to work the following day, I was informed that the suspect was later located and arrested for felony DUI and felony hit and run. One of the traffic investigators asked me if I could identify the suspect vehicle if I saw it again, and I told him that I could. The vehicle had been impounded the previous night, so I took a ride down to the impound yard with the investigator to identify the pickup truck. I noted the front-end damage on the vehicle and thought it was amazing how much damage a human body could do to such a solid object.

One day, while working at the front desk of the police department, one of the dayshift sergeants told me to go to the rooftop of city hall. I asked why I needed to go there, and he told me that someone was waiting for me up there. I thought that was a strange request but nonetheless obeyed the sergeant's directive. I went down to the basement of the police station and walked through the underground tunnel which leads to city hall. I rode the elevator to the top floor of city hall and took the stairs the rest of the way to the rooftop. When I arrived on the roof, I saw that one of our police helicopters had landed atop the helipad that was located there. That is the reason there is a windsock on top of city hall.

The pilot, who was standing next to the mechanical bird, motioned me to come over to him. He asked me if I was ready to go up. I was surprised since I had asked my supervisor if I could go on a ride-a-long in the helicopter a few months earlier. He told me he would see if he could arrange it, and apparently, he had followed through with my request. After getting some preflight safety instructions, like don't walk into the tail rotor when it's in motion and jump up and down underneath the main rotor blades, we took to the air and headed over to the central part of the city.

The pilot told me that members of our Vice Unit were conducting a prostitution sting operation where one of our detectives was wearing plain clothes and was playing the part of a "john." A john is someone who tries to pick up prostitutes for the purpose of paying for sex. The detective was driving a completely unmarked, non-descript car and was picking up prostitutes on Beach Boulevard. The prostitutes would tell the detective to drive to another location, and they would negotiate a price for sexual acts. Our job was to follow the unmarked car to wherever it ended up and to wait for the signal from the detective, which was him placing his left hand out of the driver's side window and on top of the roof of the car. We would then advise the ground units who were waiting nearby that they could move in for the arrest. We flew overhead three different prostitutes, and each time it resulted in an arrest.

I was finally 20 ½ years old, and in August 1985, I went through the hiring process to become a police recruit so that I could attend the police academy. The department did an updated background investigation and sent me to a psychologist so that I could complete a pre-employment psychological evaluation. A few weeks later, Lieutenant Davis, who was in charge of the Personnel Bureau, called me into his office and told me that the psychologist had concerns that I was too naïve and didn't have a lot of life experience. I ended up having to convince Lieutenant Davis that I would be alright and that I would try to overcome those hurdles. A couple of days later, I was notified that I got the job and would start the academy on January 19, 1986. I finished out the semester at Golden West College without having earned an Associate's Degree.

I traded my dark blue cadet uniforms for khaki-colored recruit uniforms. The property officer issued me a brand new duty belt, handcuffs, wooden baton, holster, speed loaders, and a stainless steel Smith & Wesson Model 686 with a four-inch barrel. A week later, I found myself reassigned to the graveyard shift at the HBPD Detention Center until the academy started in January. I was to be one of the youngest non-lateral officers that the department had ever hired. Some of the officers told me to get physically prepared for the academy by running and doing pushups. So, that's precisely what I did. I remember being told by the personnel officer that HBPD police recruits are expected to rank within the top ten students of their academy class. Alana and I had split up about this time. Even though I was heartbroken, there was nothing to distract me from excelling in the academy.

During my time as a cadet, I learned how to swear more and started drinking more because, after all, I needed to learn how to pour them down if I was to be a police officer. I also learned how to keep my mouth shut when I became aware of some officers' marital infidelity. Even though I felt very uncomfortable being around that type of behavior and wanted nothing to do with it, I tried to mind my own business. I knew the difference between right and wrong but somehow figured there was also a grey area when an officer may have done something unethical, like accepting a free meal because of their position. However, I didn't give it much thought since I was soon going to be starting my dream job and had to devote my full attention to the upcoming police academy. I told myself I would always try to do the right thing for the right reasons. As a future peace officer, I knew that I would encounter death and traumatic events and may have to take a human life to defend myself or someone else. But I felt I was ready because of all of the exposure I already had to such things as an explorer and a cadet. I didn't dwell on such things and just wanted to get through the academy more than anything else.

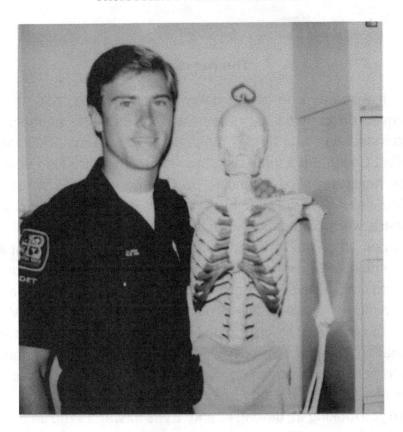

Police Cadet Keith Knotek and company, 1984.

Chapter 5

The Academy

It was day one of the police academy, and most of us arrived on campus as the sun was rising. The academy I attended was held on the campus of my alma mater, Golden West College. It served as a law enforcement training center for multiple police agencies in Orange and Los Angeles Counties. We were members of Basic Academy Class # 83. There were 59 academy recruits on that first day, and we formed up on the "grinder" in front of the flag pole as best as we could. In those days, there wasn't anything like "red guns" or training pistols. The group of us was all in uniform and carrying unloaded pistols in our holsters. Around 7:00 AM, a group of six very fit-looking uniformed tactical training officers wearing campaign hats briskly walked out onto the grinder with purpose; of stressing out as many recruits as possible. All of them were yelling terms of endearment, such as, "What are you looking at, dirtbags;" and "Eyes forward! Who said you can look at me?" They made a few of us drop and do pushups and run laps around a track. Oh, yes, it had begun. There was no doubt the police academy had started.

I remember a red-headed recruit who was sponsored by the Irvine Police Department. He was standing next to me in the formation, and during a break in between all of the yelling, he said, "I have a job waiting for me back home. I'm not doing this!" He stepped out of formation, went to the tactical staff's office, and quit. I think we lost five recruits on the first day alone. After morning formation, the academy staff made us change out of our uniforms and dress into PT gear. For the remainder of the day, we ran, did sit-ups, pushups, and the "dying cockroach." Our first day didn't end until around 7:00 pm. The tactical staff was trying their best to get more recruits to quit. Several more recruits fell out within a day or two. They just couldn't handle the physical demands and were really ill-prepared for such a rigorous program.

I was physically fit and did my best not to draw any attention to myself. I made sure my uniform was impeccable and brushed up on criminal law, radio codes, and other subject matter. The last thing I wanted to do was catch the eye of one of the tactical officers, which I had seen with a couple of the other recruits. By the second week of the academy, we had lost at least ten fellow students. On January 28, 1986, one of the academy staff members, Sergeant Baker, came into our classroom and ordered us to file out to the blacktop area in front of the flag pole called "the grinder" and to assemble in formation which we did. He announced to us that the space shuttle, Challenger, had exploded in midair and that all on board were lost. We took a moment of silence, and our class sergeant lowered the flag to half-staff.

Los Angeles Police Sergeant Richard Wemmer was our lead officer safety and survival instructor. He retired as a captain in 2008 after 40 years of service with the LAPD. He went on to become the head of security for the LA Dodgers baseball team. Sergeant Wemmer was a no-nonsense kind of guy. He was hard on us, but for a good reason. His subject matter was of the utmost importance. Sometimes a fellow recruit would raise their hand in class and want to comment on one of Sergeant Wemmer's lectures. The good sergeant would respond by saying, "Is that a question or a comment, mister? In this class, we only have time for questions!" He also said, "Do I carry a concealed weapon in church? You bet I do! It's better to have it and not need it than not to have it when you really need it!" I learned a lot from Sergeant Wemmer.

On field scenario days, some recruits would have to go to our respective agency, check out a patrol car, and drive it to the academy so that the vehicles could be used in the scenarios. I recall the days when it was my turn. I'd go to the station the night before and check out a vehicle. I remember the sense of pride and thought I was the *cat's meow* as I drove the "black & white" down the city streets. We went out to the Los Alamitos Army Airfield, which is now called Joint Forces Training Base-Los Alamitos, for our nighttime field problems. Fortunately, I did alright in my field scenarios because I had the opportunity to learn a lot of technical police procedures as an explorer and cadet.

During my last week at the police academy, one of the tactical staff officers gave me an envelope with my name on it. He said that a woman had stopped by the administrative staff office and dropped it off for me. I thanked him and opened up the envelope to see what was inside. It was a letter written by the victim of the hit and run from the previous year that Ed and I had helped. The letter said that she had healed from her injuries after months of surgeries and physical therapy. It went on to say that she was doing well and that she felt compelled by God to hunt me down at the police academy to thank me for what I did. The letter was filled with joy and gratitude, and it did my heart good to receive such an expression of jubilation. I do not know what I ultimately did with the letter, but I wish I still had it

Finally, May 16, 1986, had arrived, and it was academy graduation day. I found out my class ranking was number 11 out of 29 fellow recruits. So, I wasn't going to graduate in the top 10 of my class. I thought that that was alright; I was just happy to make it through successfully! My parents and a handful of friends were there to watch the monumental occasion. Police chiefs from the various agencies represented were there, and they conducted a final inspection of our class. My chief came down the line of recruits standing at attention. When he finally got to me, he shook my hand, congratulated me, and told me he had forgotten to bring my badge. What? No, this couldn't be! The badge pinning part of the graduation was one of the most important elements of the whole ceremony.

My friend, JB Hume, happened to be at the graduation ceremony, and he saw what was going on. He was on duty and in uniform at the time. So, he unpinned his badge from his uniform shirt and handed it to my chief to pin on me when the time came. What an honor that was to be pinned with and wear the badge of one of my most significant mentors and friends at graduation time! When academy graduation photographs were taken at the conclusion of the graduation, it was JB's badge that I was wearing. I subsequently went to the police department the next day, was sworn in, and presented with my own badge by the chief on the following day.

One of my graduation gifts was a Gonzalez, model 187 sap. A sap is a heavy chunk of lead wrapped in leather with a leather handle. It was about 10 inches long and was used as an impact weapon, kind of like a short baton. Huntington Beach PD was one of the few departments in Orange County where officers were still authorized to carry the antiquated but effective weapon. Our uniform pants had special pockets sewn into them for carrying a sap. They were called "sap pockets," but now the modern term is flashlight pockets as most law enforcement agencies have gotten away from the sap as a force option because some police administrators feel they are kind of "cave mannish" in principle.

I double-dated with an academy mate, Neil, and a couple of young ladies on graduation night. He was dating a reserve police officer from one of the local Orange County agencies, and she had a friend that was to be my blind date. Neil and I went to his girlfriend's apartment in Garden Grove and picked up the ladies. We drove to the venue in Anaheim, where our graduation dinner and academy class presentation were being held. It was a great dinner, and even better were the alcoholic beverages that were being served.

As I could feel "a buzz" from the booze I was putting into my body, one of the tactical officers from my agency, that was also getting "lit," started talking to me. I'll call him Sergeant "Smith." He was saying things to me like, "Knotek, I couldn't really screw with you too much. You just kind of blended into the herd. Your time as a cadet at the PD did you well." I thanked him, at which time another academy tactical officer from my department came over and joined the conversation. I'll call him Sergeant "Ruel." Sergeant Ruel looked at Sergeant Smith and me and said, "Come on, Knotek, let's get out of here and go drinking." I told him I couldn't because I drove to the venue and came with Neil and our dates. Sergeant Ruel said, "So, bring them along." Did I have a drinking problem? No, of course not! That's just what cops do; work hard, party harder, I thought.

Academy Class graduation photo, May 1986

Academy graduation day picture, May 1986.

Chapter 6

The Rookie

It was May 1986, and I traded in my academy "wheel gun" for a .45 caliber semi-automatic pistol. After qualifying with my new, department-issued .45, I began my field training program working uniformed patrol with an experienced field training officer or FTO. The purpose of the FTO was to teach new officers how to do their job effectively and to evaluate their performance every day. Huntington Beach PD had a history of trainees washing out of the FTO program within the first four to six months. The philosophy at the time was if a new officer can't hack the many challenges of the job, it is better just to get rid of them. My first FTO's name was Bob. He was a former Army Special Forces soldier and was a solid tactician.

Within my first few weeks on the job, I was assigned my first homicide call. I remember it so very well. Bob and I were dispatched to the Huntington Harbor area, an affluent neighborhood in the city. It was reported that a homeowner had shot his female maid to death. I was so nervous. I had been to homicide scenes before on ride-a-longs, but this was my first time as a police officer. Two officers were already on-scene and were detaining the suspect. Even though the location of the call was out of our patrol beat, as a trainee in the FTO program, I could be sent anywhere in the city to handle calls involving major crimes, such as rape, armed robbery, and murder.

Bob and I arrived on the scene in Huntington Harbor. An officer was already standing in the doorway of the residence regulating entry in and out of the crime scene. Bob and I got logged into the crime scene and entered the house. As I walked in, I saw a man seated in handcuffs on the couch in the living room to my left. The man was in his early to mid-60s, and I noticed an empty bottle of vodka and a bunch of beer bottles on the coffee table and end tables near the sofa. The suspect's speech was slurred, and his appearance was disheveled. Officer Reynolds, who had detained the suspect, motioned to me and said something to the effect of, "The dead lady is over there on the floor," as he pointed towards the kitchen.

I made my way into the kitchen area and noted a black female adult lying face down in the middle of the kitchen floor. Her body was in a large puddle of partially coagulated blood, which indicated that her body had been there for a while. I took out my notebook, began writing down my observations, and interviewed the first two officers who first arrived on the scene. Officer Reynolds told me that he and Officer Cuadras arrived first and tactically approached the residence. The homeowner, who was also the suspect, was waiting for them at the front door since he was the person who called dispatch and told them he had killed his maid. They called the suspect out of the house, detained him, and cleared the residence for any additional suspects. The homeowner apparently got into a verbal dispute with his housemaid for some unknown reason. He was so agitated that he grabbed his twelve-gauge shotgun and blasted the maid in the face and upper body, killing her. The suspect then proceeded to get even drunker and finally decided to call the police hours later.

We waited around for the crime scene investigators, detectives, and deputy coroner to arrive. I watched the deputy coroner from the sheriff's department roll over the body. The dead woman's face was pulverized and looked like it had been through a meat grinder with all of the dried blood in her hair and on her face. However, her eyes were still intact, and they were really big and wide open. To me, her eyes had the expression of I can't believe you just shot me, and now I'm going to die. At least, that was my visual and mental observation at that time.

It was like watching a bad horror movie or a very graphic television crime drama, but this happened in real life. As the new kid on the block, I got to assist the deputy coroner put the body into a brand new, clean white body bag. It was a good thing I had plenty of latex surgical gloves since the immediate scene was a bloody mess. Nonetheless, I managed to hold it together after seeing such a gruesome sight. After experiencing a few things like that within my first few months on the job, I got good at sucking it up and not talking about it with anyone.

Bob and I finished our 10-hour shift, and I went on to continue in the FTO program. The protocol in the field training program was that a trainee changed training officers monthly. So, every 30 days, I got a new field training officer. My next FTO was Officer "Cliff," and he was pretty mellow and easy-going. It was a welcome change after being under the scrutiny of Bob, who was also on the department's SWAT team. Cliff and I got into a vehicle pursuit when I was under his tutelage. It was my first as a new police officer and my first as a driver officer.

While I was still with Cliff, we were dispatched to a domestic violence call at an apartment complex. The male suspect had fled the scene prior to our arrival. I interviewed the female victim who was previously used as a punching bag by her drunk boyfriend. I gathered the information we needed for my report and took some photographs of the victim's facial injuries. I put out a "be on the lookout" call for the suspect over the radio and later filed a criminal complaint for an arrest warrant on the suspect.

A week or two later, on my days off, I ended up at one of my favorite bars in Fountain Valley, called "The Hop." As I sat at the bar drinking long island iced teas with my buddy, I heard a female voice to my left say, "Hi, officer." My first thought to myself was, *please don't let this be someone I arrested.* As I looked to my left, I saw that it was the female victim from the previously mentioned domestic violence call. She sat down on the barstool next to me, and she thanked me for my help. She even offered to buy me a drink, which I declined.

One of my FTOs, who shall remain nameless, was burning the candle at both ends. He got paid during the daytime hours to be a tactical staff officer at the police academy (I think it may have been for a reserve officer class). After working six to eight hours at the academy, he would report for work at 3:30 pm to work his 10-hour patrol assignment on the swing shift. It's needless to say he suffered from sleep deprivation and was tired during much of our time together. It was almost like working by myself when we were together because he slept in the passenger seat while I drove. He told me to wake him up if we got any radio calls. I remember going on a few "hot" calls with him involving physical fights where he had to wake up and act really fast.

I liked to drink on my days off from work. One evening I went to a bar with a couple of friends. We all got pretty lit, and I was speeding home after drinking in the bar all night. I looked in my rearview mirror and noticed the red and blue lights of a police motorcycle behind me. Oh, no! I was under the influence of alcohol and was being pulled over. As the motor officer approached my window, I recognized him. It was "Wild Bill." He recognized me too, and he said, "Hey there, cowboy, what on earth are you doing?" I told him I was driving a couple of my friends home, at which time he told me to slow down, and he let me go.

I know he smelled the alcohol on my breath, and I think he just didn't want to deal with me. So he let me go and told one of the supervisors at work. When I started my work week, I got a pretty good butt chewing from one of the sergeants. He explained to me that as a probationary police officer who was still in training, I could be fired without any explanation given. I acknowledged him, was grateful I wasn't getting a written reprimand, and told him it would never happen again. Another issue I had as a young twenty-something-year-old cop was I had a lead foot. That factor, in conjunction with my newfound love for alcohol, was a bad combination. Did I have a drinking problem? No, I just liked drinking like other officers I knew. I wasn't hurting anybody.

I was doing a satisfactory job in the FTO program; not stellar, but passable. I went on some more exciting and traumatic calls and learned a lot from my field training officers. I was sent back to dayshift after my stint on swing shift and graveyard shift concluded. My latest FTO was an officer who had been given the nickname "Jingles." I do not know why he was dubbed with that particular name, but I'm sure there was some backstory. Jingles was a no-nonsense FTO who had previously lateralled to Huntington Beach PD from a police agency in Los Angeles County. He had a lot of experience and street smarts. I learned a lot from him.

On one of my days off from work, I decided to meet up with one of my officer friends at the department's pistol range. It was an outdoor range, and as officers, we had keys to the gate. Guys would often use the range as an after-hours party place or a place to camp out in their motorhomes if they found themselves in the doghouse at home. My buddy and I barbecued and drank beer that night. He called it a night and was going to sleep in his van. I, on the other hand, decided to drive home.

As I pulled out of the parking lot at the range, I got lit up by the "night sun." Our police helicopter was flying overhead of my vehicle and the flight officer shined the 15 million candlepower spotlight (sometimes referred to as the night sun) on my car. I thought he was just saying hello as it was a well-known fact that off-duty officers would sometimes frequent the property. In my immature 21-year-old mind, I thought it would be funny to toy with the flight crew. It was after midnight, and there wasn't much traffic on the streets. So I drove really fast all of the way home with the helicopter following me.

When I went back to work, I started hearing rumors that word had gotten out about my off-duty shenanigan, and it wasn't well received. Then I remembered that the gyroscope binoculars onboard the helicopter was powerful enough to read license plates. The aircraft was also equipped with Forward Looking Infra-red (FLIR), also commonly known as night vision. They must have read my plate and ran it through DMV. Oh, well. No harm, no foul. I had seen other officers pull some really ridiculous stunts over the years, which made my actions look like small peanuts in comparison.

It was the second day of my new work week, and I was attending the morning patrol briefing for dayshift. While all of the other officers were assigned their patrol beats for the shift, the sergeant assigned me to the front desk. That had never happened before. It's not like my FTO called in sick, and there were no other FTOs to assign me to. Jingles was seated right next to me in the briefing room. After the briefing was over, I went up to the front desk and relieved the graveyard shift officer. After about an hour, another dayshift patrol officer came to the front desk. He was called in from the field to relieve me. Just then, a lieutenant came out to the desk and told me to report downstairs to the training sergeant's office.

I got a lump in my throat as I took the elevator ride down to the department's basement. I thought to myself, am I going to get a written reprimand for the stunt I pulled involving the helicopter the other night? I walked into the training sergeant's office, and Sergeant "Val" told me, "Let me see your duty weapon." I thought that was a really strange request, but I unholstered my Sig Sauer, model P220, .45 caliber pistol, dropped the magazine, and cleared my weapon. As I handed him the unloaded pistol, and before I could take a seat, he asked, "Do you carry a backup?" I nodded in the affirmative, at which time he said, "Let me see it." I retrieved my Walther PPK/S from my ankle holster, cleared it, and gave it to Sergeant Val. I knew at that point that I was in really big trouble!

Sergeant Val told me to "sit down" in a stern tone. He told me that my two off-duty screw-ups did not go unnoticed and that since I was not a superstar trainee, I was being separated from employment with the department. He said that it could go one of two ways. I could either salvage what was left of any hopes of a career in law enforcement by resigning, or he would serve me with a notice of probationary dismissal. Since the latter was essentially the same as being fired, I opted to type my resignation.

Sergeant Val handed me a department memorandum form and pointed at a typewriter located on an adjacent desk. I knew what to do. I sat down at the desk and typed, "I, Keith Knotek, hereby submit my resignation as a police officer with the Huntington Beach Police Department for personal reasons. This resignation is effective immediately upon my submission of this document." That was it; I was done. I handed in my resignation to Sergeant Val, and he asked me for my badge and department identification card. I worked so hard to get that badge, but I had lost it through my stupidity and immaturity. As I returned my entire cache of department-issued property and uniforms, I wondered what I was going to tell my family and friends.

I drove home early from my shift like a whipped puppy with my tail between my legs. This was the worst thing to ever happen to me personally. I have heard of guys getting canned on probation, and they are "blackballed" from ever getting another job in law enforcement. I was only 21 years old. How was I going to explain to a future employer that I was an officer with probably one of the most prestigious and respected agencies in Orange County, and I only lasted four months there? My only saving grace is that I was allowed to resign "for personal reasons," and hopefully, my alcohol-induced escapades would not be revealed as it showed a complete lack of good judgment on my part.

Huntington Beach Police Chief Earle Robitaille
presents Keith with his badge.

Chapter 7

Post Rookie Time

After I had let a month pass, I called an academy mate and friend who worked for a community college district police department located in Los Angeles County, which had about 10 or 12 sworn officers. I told him what had happened at Huntington Beach PD and asked him if he thought I could get hired at his agency. He told me there was an open police officer position there and that he would run it through his supervisor. About a week later, he called me and told me that his chief wanted me to submit a resume and application for the open position, which I happily did. Could this be my opportunity to get back into the profession? During this time, I also cut way back on my alcohol consumption. I was not an everyday drinker at that time but had a propensity for overdoing it when I did drink alcoholic beverages.

I subsequently went in for an interview with the chief and the one and only lieutenant. I had answers to all of their questions and seemed to have a good dialogue going with both of them. They told me that it was a major benefit to them that I was already academy trained and certified as a California peace officer. That meant they wouldn't have to send me to another police academy. But they had concerns about the circumstances and manner in which I left HBPD. We talked about it, and I assured them it was a maturing process and a learning experience for me. They had me exit the chief's office for a few minutes, and I was invited back in. The chief told me he was going to offer me a conditional offer of employment pending my successful completion of the hiring process.

I was so elated I would get to start doing what I had dreamt of doing since I was a young kid. Granted, it was campus law enforcement and not as high speed as working for a municipality or county, but it was uniformed policing. It wasn't a busy place to work, but I got to learn and practice more good patrol tactics by listening to some of the older and more senior officers. I did a really accelerated FTO program and passed with flying colors. I was able to make arrests, write citations, and conduct traffic stops, all without being under the supervision of an FTO. Was this a coming of age moment? Perhaps so.

One day, while assigned to dayshift, I received a report of a suspect being detained by a professor for commercial burglary. Apparently, the suspect, who was a Hispanic kid, about 18 or 19 years old, had broken into several classrooms on the previous night. One of the classrooms was a science lab, and all of the Pyrex test tubes, containers, and glassware were stolen. Now, why would anyone in their right mind steal that stuff? Meth; that's why! "Speed freaks!" They manufacture and smoke methamphetamine using the glassware, and I knew exactly why the kid targeted the science lab.

I don't remember how the professor figured out it was that kid who burglarized the building, but I took custody of him and drove him to our station. I read the kid his Miranda Rights, and he agreed to talk to me. He admitted to me that he did, in fact, commit the burglary. Somehow, he also ended up confessing to me that an acquaintance of his was making meth and selling it. This case snowballed into something bigger. I worked the case as far as it would take me, and I drove the young man to the LA County-Norwalk Sheriff's Station for booking.

Since all of our arrest reports had to be reviewed by an LA County Sheriff's watch commander, usually with the rank of lieutenant, I waited my turn and entered the watch commander's office. After reviewing my report, the lieutenant told me it was one of the best, well-written, and thorough reports he had seen in a long time. He told me he was going to forward my report to their narcotic enforcement team to follow up on the manufacturing and sales crimes. The lieutenant told me if I ever decided to leave college policing that, I should consider a career with the Los Angeles County Sheriff's Department. I was elated; what a nice compliment! However, that would mean I'd have to attend their in-house academy for another six months and then be assigned to jail duties for a few years after academy graduation. No thanks.

Working for the community college district allowed me to learn and grow in a less fluid environment. When I worked the graveyard shift, another officer and I would practice doing high-risk traffic stops because there was no one else on campus to get in our way. I made quite a few pedestrian checks on individuals who would come onto campus after midnight. There was no reason for them to do so because school was not in session at 2:00 am. I made some warrant arrests and was really getting the hang of policing, which also built up my self-confidence.

Cerritos Community College District Police,
1985 Jeep Cherokee police car.

Chapter 8

The Laguna Beach Days

After working for the community college district for a little more than a year, I decided that I wanted to do more. Campus policing wasn't exciting enough to satisfy my 22-year-old need for adrenaline rushes. I had kept in touch with an academy mate who went by the nickname of "Wojo." He went to work for the Laguna Beach Police Department after graduating from the academy. Laguna Beach is a 10 square mile city with a population of about 25,000 residents. There were many celebrities living in Laguna Beach at that time, including Kent McCord, Harriet Nelson, Buzz Aldrin, Bette Midler, and even OJ and Nicole Simpson before the tragic murder of Nicole. Wojo was doing really well there and was making a good name for himself at LBPD. He asked me to do a ride-a-long with his agency and to submit my application. I later ended up doing both with his encouragement.

This was also around the same time I ended up meeting and dating my future wife, who I will call Kaleigh. She was introduced to me by a mutual friend, George, who worked with her at the now-defunct Orange County Marshal's Office. I fell in love with her and thought this was the one. It was a whirlwind courtship as we ended up getting married in January 1988. I didn't know the first thing about women, relationships, and certainly not the art and science of being a husband, or at least a good one.

I ended up going through the testing process at LBPD and eventually submitted my resignation to my current employer. I was grateful they gave me an opportunity when I needed it the most. I was hired as a Laguna Beach police officer in September 1987. I still had a very youthful appearance and looked like I had stolen my uniform from a "real" policeman. I started in Laguna Beach PD's FTO program and not only passed while exceeding their standards but I was released a month early to go on solo patrol by myself.

During my career at LBPD, I experienced a lot of traffic collision deaths as Laguna Canyon Road and Pacific Coast Highway was well-known for bad traffic accidents and fatalities. I handled suicides, despondent people, robberies, a lot of burglaries, DUIs, rapes, vehicle pursuits, and just about anything else you can imagine. I gained so much valuable law enforcement experience in Laguna Beach that I could take with me anywhere. I was even appointed as an interim fill-in FTO and started training new officers.

I also continued to suppress all of the horrible trauma that I had been exposed to. I could have talked to people about it but didn't. As police officers, we are trained to push it down and move on to the next call for service. There is no time to process all of that agony and gut-wrenching stress in a ten or 12-hour shift. So, we go home to our families and do not talk about it because we don't want to burden them with the ugly parts of the job. We repeat this cycle day after day and night after night. It seemed to be working for me as I didn't feel stressed out or depressed in any way.

One evening in 1988 or 1989, I was dispatched to an injury traffic collision on Laguna Canyon Road near El Toro Road. I was either the first or the second officer to arrive on the scene, and it looked as if the two involved vehicles had collided head-on with each other. One of the cars was a Volvo station wagon. I quickly ran up to the Volvo to assess the driver's condition. When I got to the shattered driver-side window, I saw what appeared to be a female slumped towards the left. There was a gurgling sound coming from her throat, and her eyes were rolled back. I checked her for a pulse and was unable to locate one. But her face was so badly distorted that there was no way I could have even attempted to open an airway to do rescue breathing.

There were 8 X 10 glossy glamour photos of the women strewn about the inside of her car, and some had flown out of the window and landed on the highway upon impact. The photos pictured a beautiful woman who appeared to be in her late 20s or early 30s. I learned that she was apparently a model and worked for an agency that did major advertising for some of the large clothing companies. There was nothing that any of the first responders or I could have done to save her. She was dead when I found her, and that memory stays with me to this day.

One summer night in 1989, I made a vehicle stop on a traffic violator at South Coast Highway and Mountain Road. Officer Mike Jeffries pulled in behind me and exited his patrol car to see if I needed assistance with anything. I told him that I was "code 4," which is the police radio code for "no further assistance required." I let the driver go with a verbal warning, and Mike and I stood on the side of the road and talked for a bit. The backdrop for my traffic stop was a bar, as we were in an area with a handful of drinking establishments. There were a lot of pedestrians out and about that evening as it was a beautiful, balmy summer night.

As Mike and I were chatting next to our patrol cars, the bang of POP-POP could be distinctly discerned from the noise of a car backfiring. Almost simultaneously, Mike and I heard the sound of bullets whizzing past us. I had just been shot at for the first time in my career as a police officer! Mike and I crouched down behind the engine blocks of our patrol cars to give us some cover and concealment from any additional rounds that may be headed our way. It was eerie! The busy street cleared out, and all of the pedestrians disappeared and headed for cover inside the drinking establishments that were open for business.

I called for additional units to assist us, and we proceeded to conduct a two-block radius search for any shooter that may be in the immediate area, but to no avail. In retrospect, I think that someone had shot at us from a passing vehicle driving by the traffic stop scene. After my graveyard shift, Kaleigh and I went on a road trip vacation to the San Francisco Bay area as if nothing had happened at all.

Kaleigh, who had started a new job as a dispatcher with the Orange County Sheriff's Department and I attended church together on Sundays. We went to Calvary Chapel in Laguna Hills. Since I worked the graveyard shift on Saturday nights and into Sunday mornings, I would meet Kaleigh at church after I got off duty. It was really difficult for me to stay awake as I sat in church after working all night. However, the pastor was a gifted man of God, and I enjoyed his messages.

Unfortunately for me, I still had no real relationship with God, even though I believed in the Holy Trinity. My understanding of God's nature and spirituality went out the window as soon as I walked out of the church after Sunday service. I saw people who seemed genuinely happy and talked about the Holy Spirit speaking to them. I wanted what they had, but I didn't really know how to get it. My problem was that I wouldn't stay still long enough to let God work in my life. I was so grounded in the world and my own selfish interests that I had to be the one in charge of my destiny. It wouldn't be until three decades later that I finally found what I was looking for.

During the summer of 1989, I got trained on a *quad-runner* all-terrain vehicle (ATV) to work on our beach patrol detail on my days off from regular street patrol. The best part of it, besides the scenery and wearing a modified uniform with shorts, was the fact I was getting paid overtime to do it. I also worked on my suntan but usually got sunburned by the end of the day.

When people ask me, "What is the funniest thing that happened to you during your career," I'll always remember the "laundromat incident" as being high on my list. One afternoon while on patrol, I received a radio call of a drunk and disorderly male at a laundromat who was trying to pick fights with some of the patrons. I responded to the call and arrived before my back unit. When I went inside the business, I saw a Hispanic male staggering toward me. I told him to stop and not come any closer to me when he began swearing in Spanish. His eyes were bloodshot and watery, and he reeked of booze. He was obviously intoxicated, so I had already made up my mind that he was going to take the ride to jail.

When my backup officer arrived, we tried to get him to comply with being handcuffed. But he instead decided to take a swing at us. It was like a scene from a cartoon where the villain keeps swinging but misses because he is disoriented. The other officer, Matt, took the suspect down to the ground, and I moved in to try to place handcuffs on the man. But the man was kicking and flailing his legs and was hard to get a hold of. Matt and I decided I would control the guy's leg and that Matt would kneel on the suspect's back and handcuff him. I grabbed onto both legs, at which time I lost my balance and almost fell backward.

Matt got the handcuffs on the drunk and started laughing as I had a confused and panicked look on my face. In my hands, I was holding one of the man's legs. It caught me so off guard because I wasn't expecting the brave and intoxicated boxer to have a prosthetic leg. We finally lifted the man on his one good leg and helped him into the backseat of my car. He took the ride in my backseat while his leg rode in the trunk all the way to jail. That is something I still laugh about today, not because of the man's disability, but because of Matt's humorous reaction and my short-lived confusion.

One night in June of 1990, shortly after clearing patrol briefing, the radio chattered with the usual "police talk," and I was looking for potential DUI drivers on Pacific Coast Highway. Some of the other units were already sent on calls for service. One of the calls was a loud noise complaint at a large party in the south end of the city. As I searched for my next traffic violator, one of the officers, Matt, got on the radio with an excited, elevated voice and said, "Code 3 unit." That's all he could put out over the radio. Code three means to respond in emergency mode using lights and siren. As the dispatcher tried to raise him, Matt said, "Physical," which in "police speak" means he's in a fight. Several other units and I quickly responded to the party call where Matt was now putting out a call for emergency help. When I arrived, I could see a mob of people on the highway and in an apartment complex parking lot where the party was being held.

Five of us arrived on the scene within a short period of time and began to clear out the crowd. Matt was alright and managed to take control of the guy who squared off on him. Some of the crowd went to the opposite side of the highway and started congregating in a 7-11 convenience store parking lot. A decorative concrete island in the store's parking lot contained rocks and other landscaping material. Members of the crowd began to throw rocks and hurl bottles across the street at us as we were trying to manage the scene and get the situation under control.

There was an individual at the party named Kevin Anthony Dunbar, who was on parole and was also known to police because he was belligerent and always liked to fight when contacted by members of law enforcement. It turned out that Mr. Dunbar had several warrants for his arrest, so one of the officers tried to place him under arrest, at which time the fight was on. The officer went down on the sidewalk with Dunbar, and two more officers joined in the melee in an attempt to place Dunbar in handcuffs.

I could see that Dunbar had tucked his arms underneath his body in an attempt not to be placed in cuffs. He was flailing his legs, and people were still throwing objects in our direction. I made the decision to kick him in his right arm twice to try to distract him to the point that the other officers could get control of his arms and get Dunbar handcuffed. As I kicked Dunbar, I simultaneously said, "Put your hands back there, you (expletive)!" We eventually got everything under control and loaded the folks that were going to jail into our cars, including Dunbar. We booked everybody into jail and finished our shift with no further major incidents.

It was now December 1990, and the department finally decided to send me to Field Training Officer School at the San Diego County Sheriff's Training Facility. I was really pleased. I thought this was going to be my chance to promote and become a permanent FTO. The course was a week-long, and I stayed in a hotel near what was then Miramar Naval Air Station, where "Top Gun" School was located. One of our officers, Johnny, lived in Oceanside, which wasn't too far from where I was staying. After class one night, I drove to his house to have dinner with Johnny and his wife.

During my visit, Johnny told me that a video had surfaced that potentially showed a Laguna Beach police officer possibly using excessive force during an arrest. He said he thought the officer in the video was me. I started thinking back on what I could have possibly done that could have been construed as excessive force. I made a few phone calls to people at the department when one of them gave me a message to call the deputy police chief at home. I called the deputy chief, who told me that a videotape had surfaced with me in it and that the "victim's" attorney had filed a citizen complaint. I was told to complete my FTO school and that there would be an internal affairs investigation into the incident when I returned to work from San Diego.

My heart sank! I called Kaleigh and told her what was going on. She didn't really know what to say, but it no doubt caused her significant stress. I continued going to my class and would just sit in my hotel room in the evenings. On my last night of class, I called Kaleigh from my hotel room telephone. There were no such things as cell phones back then. Kaleigh told me she had just seen me on the evening news and that a portion of the mysterious video was shown. My actions looked horrible on video unless the viewer knew all of the details of the incident. For the second time in my life, I had the feeling my career in law enforcement was over.

It was January 1991, and the first Gulf War popped off while I was assigned to ride a desk at the police department. Kaleigh and I celebrated our third wedding anniversary as I endured a five-month-long internal affairs investigation. This was during a time when the old-fashioned VHS video cameras were becoming popular. As various law enforcement-related incidents were being video-taped by the average citizen across the nation, I was vilified in the media. The Rodney King incident involving the LAPD hit the news about two months after mine did, and they continued to give my incident air time along with the Rodney King Incident.

I was finally placed on paid administrative leave in March 1991, during the final stages of the internal affairs investigation. My attorney called me and informed me that the Orange County District Attorney's Office had completed their criminal investigation and determined there was no evidence that I had committed any crimes. Therefore, they were not going to file criminal charges against me. I thought that was great and that I'd soon be returning to work. The following day I received a phone call from Sergeant Workman to come down to the station and report to the Chief's office.

I was so excited I thought the Chief was going to inform me that the investigation was over and to start back on patrol. I couldn't have been more mistaken than I had thought. I walked into the Chief's office and was told to take a seat. There was another sergeant in the room. The Chief told me that even though I didn't commit any crimes, he felt my use of a kicking technique that I was taught in the police academy was inappropriate under the circumstances. He further stated that my use of force was not consistent with the "philosophy" of the Department's use of force policy and that he had "political realities" to consider. Therefore, he was terminating my employment as a police officer. I felt there was no coming back from this, and I would have to consider a new career path. Maybe I wasn't meant to be a cop. Perhaps I have more to mature and learn if I was to ever continue in the profession.

Keith being sworn in and received his badge from
Chief Neil Purcell in 1987.

Keith on a traffic stop in 1988.

Beach patrol, circa 1989.

Chapter 9

The Interim Period

After being fired and collecting unemployment benefits, I decided to go back to college to finish up my Associate's Degree. I began to take general education courses at Saddleback Community College in Mission Viejo in order to fulfill the math, physical sciences, and history requirements for a degree. During this time, Kaleigh and I decided that we wanted to leave Orange County and start a family near her parents in Shasta County, located in the far northern part of California. This was a time for self-reflection, reinvention, and change.

Kaleigh applied to be a dispatcher with the Shasta County Sheriff's Department, and I applied to be a deputy sheriff with the same agency. Kaleigh was subsequently hired into the dispatch position and made the move north. I was finishing the college semester and would be joining her after I was done. From November to December of 1991, I was devoted to a life of academia while living on my own. Before the end of the semester, I was notified by the personnel officer at the Shasta County Sheriff's Department that they would not even consider me for a position in their department while I was suing the City of Laguna Beach for wrongful termination.

I finished the semester and headed up to Redding, where I joined Kaleigh in our new apartment. It was right before Christmas, and the weather in Shasta County was much colder than it was in balmy Orange County. On Christmas Eve 1991, Kaleigh told me to sit down in the living room because she had something she wanted to show me. I wondered to myself, what is this all about? I sat down, and Kaleigh pulled something out from behind her back. She showed it to me and asked, "What do you suppose this means," while pointing to the big plus + sign on the pregnancy kit.

Oh my gosh, I'm going to be a dad! But I'm not ready to be a dad, I thought. I was currently unemployed at that time and had no good job prospects lined up. I had about eight months to figure something out. "Holy cow," I exclaimed! Needless to say, my fearful and insensitive reaction to the news did not go over well with Kaleigh. What should have been a joyful moment ended up with me wanting to fix the situation and control my own future. I did not lean on the Lord but instead took matters into my own hands. I was happy but also scared to death at the same time.

I needed a job, and I needed one fast. I really wanted to get back into law enforcement if there was even a slight chance to do so. I decided to drop my wrongful termination lawsuit against the City of Laguna Beach so that I could pursue my desire to get hired by a law enforcement agency. I called the personnel officer with the Shasta County Sheriff's Department and informed him that I had dropped my lawsuit. I later received a letter in the mail inviting me to attend an oral interview for a deputy sheriff position with the county. But my unemployment benefits were running out, and I needed a steady income. I knew that it would take a while to go through the sheriff's department's hiring process if I passed my interview.

I got a job as a graveyard shift hospital security officer at Redding Medical Center in the interim. I felt that it was so demeaning because, after all, security guards were people who were either fired from law enforcement or couldn't get hired by an agency in the first place. The pay was meager, and the hours were horrible. However, I needed the income and was able to get the job reasonably quickly. Kaleigh worked dayshift as a dispatcher at the sheriff's department, and I would sleep during the day after working my graveyard shifts at the hospital.

I ended up going to my interview at the Shasta County Sheriff's Department and subsequently passed every component of their hiring process, including the background investigation. I provided the background investigator with Laguna Beach's internal affairs investigation transcripts. They were about 10 inches thick and contained volumes of information. But the background investigator thoroughly read the transcripts and interviewed multiple former co-workers from LBPD. I was told that the Sheriff reviewed my background file and felt that my firing from LBPD was purely a political termination. This was great news! However, the bad news was that the County of Shasta was in a budget crisis, and they implemented a hiring freeze. My hiring was deferred, and I continued to work as a security guard.

I don't remember how I heard about it. But I discovered that the Whiskeytown National Recreation Area, which was just west of Redding, had federal law enforcement officers that patrol the park. By this time, it was March of 1992. One day I decided to take a drive to Whiskeytown to go on a fact-finding mission. I went to the ranger station and spoke with the dispatcher/clerk at the front counter, who called in a patrol ranger from the field for me to talk to. The ranger's name was Alan, and he was a supervisory ranger in the law enforcement division at Whiskeytown. He handed me the longest application for employment that I have ever seen and told me to fill it out. There were several open seasonal law enforcement ranger positions that needed to be filled for the summer season.

The fact that the Shasta County Sheriff's Department greenlighted my background gave me hope that I could get a federal law enforcement commission as a National Park Service Ranger. I completed my application and returned it to Alan, who forwarded my application to the personnel officer. About a month later, Alan called me at home and told me that my application had been preliminarily approved. I was invited to a pre-employment interview with the park superintendent. I went on to be interviewed by an agent from the U.S. Office of Personnel Management and completed the hiring process. In early May 1992, Alan called me and told me that my hiring was approved and to come into the ranger station to be outfitted with uniforms and equipment. This was great as Kaleigh, and I were expecting our first child around August or September. The higher pay would undoubtedly be welcomed.

I couldn't believe it; I was back in the saddle again. I gave the hospital notice that I had accepted a new position, and I received my badge and firearm. I was issued a Smith & Wesson, Model 19 revolver. I hadn't carried a "wheel gun" since the academy. *Man was the Park Service backward with some of their equipment*, I thought. But I didn't care all that much. I was just grateful to obtain another position in law enforcement finally.

I loved working for the Park Service! It was indeed a beautiful environment in which to work. I got to see bears, bald eagles, and mountain lions on a regular basis. The season was actually pretty busy, with all of the people from the San Francisco Bay Area visiting the lake and campsites during the summer. I made a lot of arrests, got in several vehicle chases, and had a couple of scuffles with people I was trying to arrest. My previous law enforcement experience in the city made me a more effective park ranger. I learned how to work alone in a remote area where backup was not easily accessible. This forced me to learn how to talk to people more effectively instead of escalating bad situations into something worse.

It was early September 1992, and I started getting worried because the summer season was ending, and I would soon be out of a job. I didn't know what I was going to do. I didn't want to go back to work at the hospital. One day before the season ended, I received a phone call from Sergeant Kingsley, the personnel supervisor at the sheriff's department. He told me that the county's hiring freeze had been lifted and offered me a position as a deputy sheriff. I couldn't believe it; all of my worries were quashed. I met with Sheriff Pope and Undersheriff Schaller prior to starting with the sheriff's department. They were wonderful Christian men, and they welcomed me into the sheriff's department family. I will start my new position in late September. Did I thank God for such a gift? No, probably not. I was too busy running my own life to think about God.

It was September 10, 1992, and I had to appear in U.S. District Court in Redding regarding an arrest I had made. As I sat in the galley of the courtroom, I saw a court clerk come out of a side door. She approached the other clerk that was seated next to the judge, Federal Magistrate Richard Bay, and handed her a note. That clerk gave the judge the message, at which time the judge paused and read the note. Judge Bay asked, "Is Ranger Knotek here?" I raised my hand and said, "Here, your honor." Judge Bay blindsided me and said, "Your wife is in labor. Go!" He motioned me to leave the courtroom, which I hastily did.

I drove hastily back to the ranger station to turn in the patrol car. I called Kaleigh when I got to the station to find out what was happening. She told me she went to her doctor's appointment and found out she was dilating and was about to go into labor. She further explained that I needed to get home fast so that I could pick her up and drive to the hospital. I'll admit, I was freaking out a bit as this was all new for me. I made the drive home and then to Mercy Medical Center.

We decided if it were a girl, we would name her Alexandra Elizabeth Knotek. I was with Kaleigh the entire time of the birth. While the baby was being delivered, the doctor said, "The baby is in distress!" Oh, no. The umbilical cord was wrapped around the baby's neck and was preventing the baby from breathing. The doctor reacted quickly and successfully delivered a baby girl. We welcomed Alexandra into the world, and our lives were forever changed. Every fear that I had about being a father went out the window when I saw my baby girl for the first time.

I took a week off of work and helped Kaleigh as best as I could. We adjusted to the new addition to our family, and I followed Kaleigh's lead when it came to doing "baby stuff." Sheriff Pope and Undersheriff Schaller actually had flowers delivered to our apartment to congratulate us. I thought if everybody in the sheriff's department was as thoughtful as the Sheriff and Undersheriff, I was going to love working there.

I returned to work at the Park Service for the last two weeks of the season and started with the Shasta County Sheriff's Department in late September. I was assigned to the Main Jail Facility on Court Street in Downtown Redding. I didn't really like working in the jail after working patrol. After all, I was a 27-year-old adrenaline junkie and needed to chase "bad guys." But I was just blessed to have the opportunity. Another blessing was that the Park Service wanted to keep me on as an intermittent employee to fill in when during vacation or sick time relief. I got special approval from

Undersheriff Larry Schaller to do so. That would never have happened in today's climate. There would have been the whole conflict of interest and federal/state law enforcement authority issues. But I was happy to fill in at the park on some of my days off from the sheriff's department.

I worked for the Shasta County Sheriff's Department for almost two years. I found myself getting the wanderlust again. I felt I needed to get back in the field as a full-time patrol officer. One of our deputies that I worked with in the jail, Kory, had laterally transferred to the Butte County Sheriff's Office (BCSO), which was located two counties southeast of Shasta County. Kory and I kept in touch. He loved it at BCSO, and he encouraged me to apply. Kory said it was a busy department and that there was a lot of activity out on patrol. He told me that he was assigned his own take-home, marked patrol car after he got out of the FTO program. Wow, I thought this was great. So I submitted an application to be a deputy sheriff at BCSO. Kory ended up doing very well for himself, and he is currently the elected Sheriff of Butte County.

From L to R: Rangers Ted Hoffman, Keith Knotek, Matthew Krichner, and Paul Stone, 1993.

Chapter 10

Butte County

I was hired as a deputy sheriff in Butte County in December 1993. Butte County Sheriff's deputies are also cross-trained as deputy coroners and are dispatched to death investigation calls anywhere within the county. So that certainly added a new element to my job duties. During my first week on the job, I spent time with the administrative sergeant, Larry Estes. He drove me around the county and showed me the vast area our deputies patrolled. Sergeant Estes issued me a bunch of equipment and introduced me to many key individuals I would have frequent contact with later on. Larry was promoted a couple of years later and became a lieutenant. He was a wealth of knowledge and had been working for BCSO since he was honorably discharged from the U.S. Navy.

I went through the FTO program and was later assigned to the Court Services Division. After my 6-month stint of being the bailiff for the presiding judge of Butte County Superior Court in Oroville, I was notified that I was being reassigned to patrol in the Chico area, or what we called *north county patrol*. I worked the 5:00 pm to 3:00 am shift. It was busy, and it was fun! It satisfied my need for action and excitement. Kaleigh took a job as a dispatcher in the department. So we were indeed a BCSO family. We tried to work opposite shifts so that one of us could be home to take care of little Alexandra.

Within my first year at BCSO, I was dispatched to an audible burglary alarm call at a ranch-style house in the country. As I tried to enter the property stealthily, I came upon a chain-link fence and a front gate. As I opened the gate and got about two steps into the front yard, I saw movement on the right side of the house. It was a Billy goat, and it was charging at me full speed. I thought I'd just talk nicely to it, like a dog. I said, "Good boy, nice goat," like I was happy to see it. But when the goat got close, it tried ramming me with its forehead. I took a step backward and again said, "Nice goat!" Then the goat got on its hind legs and pushed off of me with its front legs. My clean uniform was now covered in dirt. So, there I was, looking like an idiot because someone's goat attacked me. It's a good thing no one saw what had happened. I decided that if that goat didn't allow me to set foot on the property, it surely would not allow a burglar to come into its yard. I ended up getting in my car and driving away. This full-on hillbilly experience was an affirmation that I was no longer working in an urban area.

One evening before Christmas Eve, I was parked on East Avenue and State Highway 32 near the City of Chico, monitoring traffic for speeders. I saw a car traveling southbound on Highway 32, and it was coming right at me. The driver began to flash the headlights at me. At first, I thought, *what is this guy doing*? Then I realized the driver was frantically trying to get my attention. As the car came pulling up to my location, the lady behind the steering wheel told me there was a horrible traffic accident a couple of miles up Highway 32. Since the accident occurred on a state highway in an unincorporated area, it fell within the jurisdiction of the California Highway Patrol. Unbeknownst to me, CHP already had units responding to the crash along with emergency medical personnel, but I advised my dispatch that I was also en route to see if I could help.

I was the first emergency responder to arrive on the scene, and I saw two totaled vehicles in the middle of the highway, which appeared to be a head-on collision. I turned on my emergency overhead lights and blocked off the northbound traffic until more units could arrive and conduct traffic control. Traffic was backed up for at least a mile in both directions. I got out and started triaging the injured drivers and passengers. Everyone was banged up pretty badly, and one of the drivers appeared to be deceased. EMS arrived within about a minute after me, at which time I directed them to assist the deceased driver in case he had a weak pulse that I was unable to detect. The man was subsequently airlifted to Enloe Hospital in Chico, where he was pronounced deceased. Finally, a second and a third ambulance arrived, and EMS personnel were tending to all of the injured parties. I was saddened by what I had seen. But there was work to be done and no time for moping around and feeling blue.

Several CHP units arrived to conduct their traffic collision investigation. Even a neighboring Glenn County Sheriff's deputy arrived to assist with traffic control since the crash occurred near the Butte/Glenn County line. I noticed the vehicle containing the dead driver had a bunch of wrapped Christmas gifts in the backseat, and a female passenger was removed from that car and loaded into an ambulance. Since there was plenty of emergency personnel on-scene, I decided to go to the hospital to gather all the information I needed for my death investigation report.

I ended up in the emergency room with the corpse from the traffic accident and saw several of the injured passengers being treated by ER staff. I spoke with the female passenger, who told me that the deceased driver was her fiancé and they were to be married on New Year's Day. This would have been their first Christmas together had what turned out to be a drunk driver not crossed over into their lane and hit them head-on. I was deeply saddened by her story and the circumstances of her fiancé's death; damned drunk drivers, I thought. I noticed a couple of uniformed Glenn County Sheriff's deputies that came into the ER, and they started talking to the young lady I had just interviewed. It turns out she was a public safety dispatcher for their department, and her fiancé was a reserve deputy sheriff for Glenn County. How sad!

Another incident I remember to this day was getting dispatched to Reservoir Road in Palermo, near Oroville, on a dead baby call. When I arrived at the mobile home, there were still firefighters and paramedics there. One of the medics pointed at a bed with the tiny female infant lying lifeless on top. The medics and fire department departed from the scene and left me alone with the distraught mother. I remember feeling so uncomfortable. The baby's mother was coming apart at the seams, and I still had a death investigation to conduct. I remember thinking about my little two-year-old daughter Alexandra, and I was suddenly overcome with a feeling of deep sadness and empathy for the grieving mother. I was somewhat able to provide some comfort to her and called for one of her relatives to come over and support the woman. The medical examiner later deemed the cause of death to be sudden infant death syndrome (SIDS).

Although we patrolled the whole county and a small contract city called Biggs, several cities in Butte County had their own municipal police departments, including the City of Chico. Chico was the largest city in the county and was pretty much the retail and cultural center for the area. It is home to California State University, Chico; Bidwell Mansion; and a vibrant downtown business district. One afternoon in 1995, I was working the dayshift out of our Chico Substation when I heard our dispatch put out an 11-99 call (shots fired-officer needs help) over the radio. A Chico PD officer had been shot in the face in front of Mervyn's department store at the North Valley Plaza Mall. A description of the armed suspect was given, and he was believed to still be on foot in the area. This was an *all-hands-on-deck* type of situation.

This was the first time I've ever heard the code "11-99" used over the radio. My adrenaline shot up as I began racing to the scene with my lights and siren screaming. When I arrived in the area of East Avenue and Cohasset Road, other units were in a neighborhood just north of the shooting site. The officers broadcast that they were locking down the neighborhood to conduct yard-to-yard searches and not to let anyone in or out of the area. I took up a perimeter position at Pillsbury Road and East Avenue while several of our sheriff's K-9 units responded to assist the city officers with their search. As I did my job, I worried about the city officer who had been shot. Did I know him? Did he survive? *Will he be all right?* I thought to myself.

After about an hour, one of our K-9 handler deputies put out a broadcast that the suspect had been located and was taken into custody. I was very thankful for that, and I linked up with a Chico PD officer I knew to find out exactly what had happened. He told me that Officer Rod O'Hern, who I had known and previously assisted on a couple of incidents, responded to the Mervyn's store regarding a shoplifter that was taken into custody by store security. When Rod walked outside with the handcuffed suspect to be transported to jail, a young man, maybe 18 or 20-years-old, stepped out from behind a large concrete column and pointed a pistol at Rod.

The youngster demanded that Rod let his friend go or he would shoot him. Rod tried to talk to the kid to calm him down, but the suspect shot him in the face. The armed suspect then fled on foot. But what I cannot remember is if the shoplifter took off as well or if he remained at Mervyn's. I later learned that the suspect's pistol was loaded with snake shot, thank God! Although Rod permanently lost his vision in one of his eyes, the outcome could have been much worse had the suspect been using regular bullets. This was another harsh wake-up call that our profession is a dangerous one.

I was eventually appointed as an FTO and began to train new deputies. I was also assigned to the department's Hostage Negotiation Team as a collateral assignment. My career was starting to really take off. I was so blessed with the way God had salvaged my career and provided for my family. But I really didn't give it much thought. I was too busy trying to climb the "corporate ladder" at work to be grateful for what God had done for me. After about 18-months of working patrol, I was reassigned to a position as a designated area deputy in the Community Oriented Policing Program (COPS). My beat was an unincorporated area called Chapmantown. There were two other deputies in the COPS program. One of the deputies, Jack, was assigned to the Gridley Housing Area, and the other one, Mitch, was assigned to Southside Oroville.

Chapmantown at that time was kind of "ghetto-ish." There were a lot of criminal street gang members and what some would call "undesirables" living in the neighborhood. There were also some really wonderful, caring, and law-abiding folks living there too. I felt that it was my job to deal with the criminal element and to keep the good people safe from the bad guys. It was the classic guardian personality scenario. I learned so much during my Chapmantown assignment. It was very rewarding, and I really began to develop a genuine friendship with some of the people I served there. I encountered and talked to gang members almost on a daily basis. They even let me take pictures of them throwing up their gang signs. Little did they know their photographs went in my "gang book" next to their profile. I tried to keep track of their activity, and maintaining a historical and updated file on each gang member helped our detectives and me to solve a few cases.

Since the COPS program was a new initiative for BCSO, I had a lot of latitude to implement and develop the way I approached my duties. I was allowed to organize warrant sweeps with the other COPS deputies and to write my own search warrant affidavits instead of going through the Detective Bureau. Some members of the community donated a bicycle for me to use. I often rode the bike during the evening hours because I was able to easily maneuver and reach areas that I couldn't in a patrol car. I decided not to work a regular pattern of shifts and adjusted my working hours so that the "bad guys" wouldn't anticipate seeing me in the neighborhood at a particular time. One of the county board of supervisors members secured me some office space with my own phone line at one of the local fire stations. I freely gave my office number out to the public so that they could leave me messages and anonymous crime tips on my answering machine.

During my assignment in Chapmantown, Kaleigh told me she was pregnant with our second child. We decided that we did not want to know the gender of our future baby. So we prepared a "gender-neutral" bedroom for baby number two until she was born. Yes, she! In June 1995, Kaleigh and I were blessed with a healthy baby girl named Amanda Michelle Knotek. Alexandra was now a big sister to little Amanda. Kaleigh decorated Amanda's room in "girly" décor. In fact, Kaleigh had such a gift for painting and artistry that both of the girls' rooms were beautifully decorated. I felt really comfortable having another newborn since I already had enough practice after Alexandra was born. After the birth of Amanda, Kaleigh resigned from her position as a dispatcher so that she could be a stay-at-home mom. We felt it was best for both of our daughters to have a parent home full-time.

I was truly blessed! I wanted one boy and one girl. But after Amanda was born, I didn't care. I was so overjoyed to have a beautiful, healthy baby girl. Everything seemed to be going my way. I was excelling in my career, and I had a close to perfect family. By this time, Kaleigh and I had already purchased our first house. It was a small three-bedroom, two-bathroom home located in Oroville. I was able to work overtime in order to make up for the loss of Kaleigh's income. I felt I was doing a good job at work and had hopes of promoting to sergeant. Life just couldn't get much better than that, or so I thought.

On August 7, 1996, I was heading north on Highway 99 to my Chapmantown patrol area when I heard a deputy in Oroville broadcast over the radio that a plane was going down near the County Administration Center. Another deputy said he saw the pilot coming down on a parachute. I made a U-turn and started heading back to the Oroville area as this did not sound good. Finally, I heard another broadcast stating that the plane had crashed and exploded into the parking lot of the local newspaper building, the Oroville Mercury-Register. I could see a flume of thick black smoke as I drove to the scene.

When I arrived, I ended up being really close to the crash site. I instantly felt the heat from the fire as I got out of my car, which was an indicator that I was too close to the burning jet. I directed all of the "lookie-loos" away from the area using my patrol car's public address system and waited for further instructions from our dispatch center. We were advised that the aircraft was a U.S. Air Force U-2 spy plane out of Beale

Air Force Base in Marysville. The dispatcher told us that USAF personnel were en route to the crash site and to maintain a wide perimeter of the area.

The pilot, Captain Randy Roby, had experienced mechanical issues with the aircraft and ejected from the cockpit. Unfortunately, in doing so, he may have struck part of the plane's canopy, and he was deceased when he came down on his parachute. The military aircraft did a nose dive into the Mercury-Register's parking lot and struck a lady who had just walked out of the building after paying her newspaper bill. She was incinerated and consumed by the fire. A little bit of irony to this whole event was when the air force people showed up; they herded all of the newspaper employees that were inside of the building and loaded them into a government van. They told them they were going to be transported to sheriff's headquarters, where they would be debriefed and not to talk to anybody, especially the press. They were like, "Really? We are the press!"

Shortly after the "U-2 incident," Kaleigh told me that she didn't love me anymore and that she was leaving me. What! This could not be happening. I didn't cheat on her nor did I abuse her. All I did was work and come home, but apparently, she wanted more. Like I said before, I didn't know the first thing about being a good, caring, communicative husband. I never talked to Kaleigh about my feelings, her feelings, or the horrible things I had seen at work. How was I going to fix this problem? I was willing to do whatever it took to restore my marriage.

As it turned out, it was too late to save the marriage. We were both so young and immature when we got married. We had two young daughters, and Kaleigh decided she wanted to get her old job back at the Orange County Sheriff's

Department and move back to southern California. She told me that we could share custody of our girls every two weeks. This meant we had to pay for daycare on our workdays when we had the girls. What a nightmare. I started losing weight fast, and my hairline began to recede due to stress. In early October 1996, Kaleigh finally made the move back to Orange County. I watched my life head south in a U-haul truck. It sounds almost like an old country song.

One evening while working my Chapmantown assignment, I heard one of our north county patrol deputies, Scott Parks, getting dispatched to some type of a domestic squabble on Meier Drive in the unincorporated area of Chico. It was super busy that evening, and he didn't have a backup unit, so I left Chapmantown and told dispatch that I would respond as a secondary unit as I was only about 15 or 20 minutes away from the location of the call. Shortly after Scott arrived on the scene, he put out a "man with a gun" and then "shots fired." I began rolling with lights and siren, and Chico PD also sent some units since the call was close to the city limits.

The short version of this story is that a man had gone to his estranged girlfriend's house and got into an argument. He was already drunk, and he walked out of the house and got into his parked pickup truck that was sitting in front of the residence. When Scott arrived on the scene and started approaching the house, the man pointed a pistol out of the driver's side window and fired off a shot. Scott took cover and requested emergency backup. Now, there was an armed standoff with the man in the truck.

Since I was already on the hostage negotiation team, I called for additional support from the team. Kory, one of the team members, lived close by, and he arrived pretty quickly.

So he and I devised a plan to approach the pickup truck tactically using a ballistic shield and take cover behind one of the marked patrol cars. He would be the contact negotiator and was to be the cover officer with my pistol out. As our plan came together, I had my front gunsight honed in on the man's upper body, just below the neck. The man subsequently pointed the pistol out of the window again and fired a round off into the air. I really thought he was going to try to point the gun at one of us and get me to kill him, and I almost did. Fortunately, I saw the barrel of his handgun point up towards the sky, and that didn't happen. Kory managed to talk the guy into exiting the vehicle and putting the pistol on the hood of the truck. We subsequently moved up, and Kory tackled the man to the ground. It worked out well, and nobody was hurt. But it just as easily could have gone the other way.

I started drinking more as a way to calm my nerves. But drinking had not yet gotten in the way of life. The heavier drinking came towards the end of my career. I still held it together, went to work, and fulfilled the many responsibilities I had at the time. In late October of 1996, I was promoted to sergeant and sent to south county patrol. I was placed in charge of the nightshift patrol team in the southern geographical area of the county and was given the collateral assignment of K-9 Team sergeant. I was responsible not only for my patrol personnel but also for six deputies on the K-9 Team. This kept me really busy as I learned how to be a first-line and specialized team supervisor. Our K-9 trainer gave me a book to read about police working dogs and worked with me on learning the finer details about the world of police canines. My deputies were good about breaking me in, and I got to wear the bite suit and sleeve a lot during K-9 team training days.

I loved my new assignments. However, I was torn between my job and the responsibility of being a dad. I realized that the following year Alexandra was supposed to start kindergarten, and that would be the end of my time with the girls every two weeks as she would be attending school in Orange County. I felt I had to be a responsible father and move back to southern California to be closer to my girls. My daughters were way more important to me than my job. I applied for a position as a lateral police sergeant with the San Jacinto Police Department in Riverside County, California. It seemed that there were not enough in-house candidates that met the requirements to be a sergeant at SJPD, so they expanded their search and opened it up to outside applicants. If I were to be hired by SJPD, I could live about an hour away from where the girls were living with their mother. I was invited for an interview in San Jacinto and started their hiring process.

Keith in 1996.

1997 Butte County Sheriff's K-9 Team; pictured from L to R: Deputy Mark Hidalgo, Deputy Mike Lydon, Deputy John Muldown, Sgt. Keith Knotek, Deputy Steve Pelton, Deputy Steve Sloan, Deputy Scott Parks, and police service dogs.

Chapter 11

Randy

In the meantime, I was getting to know the men and women who worked on my team and under my supervision. To me, it was a sacred honor to be responsible and charged with the care and mentoring of such a fine group of people. In the back of my mind, I knew that I might be leaving them if I were to be hired by SJPD. As I previously mentioned, I was conflicted about leaving after just being promoted only six months earlier. But being close to my daughters was what I was supposed to do. Being an active father and participating in my girls' lives was an even higher calling. So I continued to work at BCSO while I periodically traveled south to complete the various phases of San Jacinto's hiring process.

On the afternoon of May 21, 1997, I pulled the patrol car out of my garage like I usually did and headed into work. It was an extremely busy shift, and there was a lot of radio traffic on my police radio. Some of my deputies were already in a foot pursuit of a possibly armed felon in Southside Oroville, but they had lost him in an area between two houses. So, I headed their way to coordinate for additional resources and to assist them in their search. We eventually captured and arrested the bad guy we were looking for, and the shift went on. It was so busy, and my deputies and I were running from call to call. I went on a domestic disturbance call with Deputy Randy Jennings, where a teenager was quarreling with his parents. However, the teenager had run away from home prior to our arrival at the house. Randy stayed at the house to obtain the information he needed for his report and I left and headed to the county gas pumps since my patrol vehicle was getting low on fuel.

It was now about 9:35 pm, and there didn't appear to be any end in sight regarding the calls for service that were stacking up. When I arrived at the fuel pumps, I ran into one of my deputies, Jim Norman, who was also fueling his patrol car. Jim was my eldest deputy and a rookie cop at the age of 50. He was previously a dispatcher with the department, and he decided to go to the academy and become a deputy. We made small talk, and at about 9:50 pm, Jim got a radio call of a husband chasing his wife with a gun in front of their residence on Butte Avenue. Since all of the other units were tied up on calls, I told dispatch that I would respond as Jim's backup unit. We cleared the gas pumps and headed towards Butte Avenue.

Jim and I arrived around 9:56 pm and contacted numerous children inside of the residence. We conducted a brief area check outside of the house and an interior check of the residence for the male and female involved in the dispute. But they were both nowhere to be found. I obtained a physical and clothing description from the children of the involved parties and put out a radio broadcast for any units in the area to check for the subjects. Since we had cleared the house for any threats, I told Jim to stay there and to gain additional information while I drove through the neighborhood to search for the two people in question.

Deputy Randy Jennings was not assigned to the call but had already cleared his earlier runaway juvenile call. He responded to our area and began checking for the involved parties. At approximately this time, a California Highway Patrol (CHP) unit in the area contacted Randy and advised him that he had just observed an Asian male, matching the description, running southbound on 10th Street. Randy drove his patrol unit southbound on 10th Street in an attempt to locate the suspect. When Randy reached the intersection of 10th Street and Grand Avenue (approximately two blocks from the suspect's residence), he observed an Asian male matching the description run into a field behind a church at that intersection. The field had a growth of approximately two to three feet of dried, tall grass and toward the south perimeter of the area was a group of trees.

Deputy Jennings positioned his patrol unit on the south side of the church and advised BCSO Dispatch that he was in foot pursuit of the subject, running south through the field. At approximately this time, I arrived at the church parking lot. I exited my patrol vehicle and started running into the area in an attempt to assist Randy with the foot pursuit. Randy had an approximately twenty-five to thirty yard lead on me at this point in time. I did not see a weapon in the suspect's hand but called for a K-9 unit to assist us in the foot chase.

My heart was pounding as I ran with 18 pounds of gear around my waist and tried to catch up to Randy and the suspect. Suddenly, the eerie silence was broken as the echoes of gunfire shattered the air like the sound of a lightning strike. The suspect turned and opened fire on Randy and me at this point. I first saw the muzzle flash in the darkness and heard the shots as a round passed closely by me. Then, I saw Randy go down as he was running. *Oh, my God*, Randy was hit! I thought *this couldn't be happening*, but it was indeed unfolding right in front of me. Ironically, the suspect crouched next to an olive tree located in the middle of the field to use as cover. Once known as a symbol of peace, the olive tree became an unwelcome element in this fight for life.

It almost seemed as if time had slowed down, but everything happened so very fast in reality. I put out an 11-99 call and dropped down into the tall, dry grass in order to get some concealment from the suspect's rounds. As I did so, I heard more gunfire going off. When the gunfire stopped, I popped back up to acquire the suspect's position so I could engage him with my pistol. But there was dead silence, and Randy had gone down right between the suspect and me. Now the only sound I could hear was the radio chatter and sirens off in the distance that were headed to my location.

I said the quickest silent prayer ever at that time, asking God to please get us out of there alive. I briefly thought about my daughters and began to coordinate units in the area to assist. I did not know if the suspect was hunkered down in the grass or behind an olive tree that was off in the distance. But what I did know at the time was that we needed to get to Randy, rescue him, and get him immediate medical attention. I began directing the responding units to where I needed them to go over my radio. I remember having a difficult time talking because of the stress-induced knot in my throat. Deputies Jim Norman, K-9 Deputy John Muldown, and a CHP officer arrived at the chaotic scene, and we all entered the danger area to search for the suspect and Randy. We first located the suspect, who was obviously deceased, and secured the body. We found Randy lying about 10 feet from the suspect's body, and he was non-responsive. We ripped open his uniform shirt and pulled off the front panel of his vest. It was at that time I could see a bullet wound to Randy's upper chest/lower neck area. Jim and John started CPR on Randy while I dealt with continuing to coordinate the emergency response to the scene.

Randy was airlifted via helicopter to Enloe Hospital in Chico, where he was pronounced dead. It was later determined during the course of the post-shooting investigation that Randy was struck once in the left wrist, once in the upper chest (just above the ballistic vest), and twice in the ballistic vest. Randy returned ten rounds of fire, striking the suspect twice in the mid-torso section, causing irreparable damage to the suspect's liver. Randy continued to crawl toward the suspect, at which point in time the suspect placed his own handgun against his chest and fired one round (contact wound) into his chest, instantly killing himself.

After the shooting, another deputy drove me to the station since my parked patrol car had become part of the crime scene. After my adrenaline started coming down, I remember feeling such extreme grief and sorrow. All of the personnel who were directly involved at the scene of the shooting were sequestered so that we couldn't talk to one another before being interviewed by the post-shooting investigators. As I sat in my lieutenant's office by myself, I started to feel pain on my right palm and chest. When I looked at my right hand, which also happened to be my shooting hand, I had a piece of rusty barbed wire prong stuck in my palm. When I hit the ground as the shooting started, I apparently landed on an old downed barbed wire fence. When I took my shirt and body armor off, I had a bunch of starthistle (prickly stickers) between the front panel of my vest and t-shirt. I didn't feel any of that pain when I had the adrenaline rush from being shot at. However, I became acutely aware of not only the emotional pain I was suffering but also the physical pain as the adrenaline was wearing off.

After we were all interviewed, I was driven home by my lieutenant. I couldn't sleep, and I started to feel ridden with guilt. Three of us ran into that field, and I was the only one to make it out alive. Now I know there wasn't anything else I could have done, but back then, I felt that I was responsible for Randy's safety as his supervisor and as a fellow law enforcement officer. I started experiencing "survivor's guilt" I just sat in my house all alone and cried. After the morning sun had risen, I heard a knock on my front door. It seemed that two off-duty deputies wanted to commiserate and greave with me. I let them in, and we told each other Randy stories. It just so happened that they brought a couple of bottles of hard liquor with them. So we drank until it was all gone.

After the guys left, I decided I needed to try to get some sleep as I was beyond exhausted. As I lay on my bed and started to drift off to sleep, I was abruptly awakened by gunfire in my head. I woke up in distress until I realized it was only a dream. I had developed post-traumatic stress and didn't yet really realize it. I was off work for two weeks until the County's contract psychologist could clear me to go back to work. I just sucked it up and told him that I was fine and that the murder of my friend wouldn't affect my performance on the job. I did not know myself very well back then.

Randy was a true gentleman and a fine person. I'm not just saying that because of the way he died so tragically. He loved his wife and family so very much. He was a SWAT team member and had been made deputy of the year the previous year. I had just written his annual performance evaluation and got to read some of the letters of appreciation in his personnel file that citizens sent in to thank Randy for some of the good, professional services that he provided them. About a month before the shooting, Randy and I were eating together in a local restaurant when he shared his belief in Jesus with me. This gave me comfort, and I knew where Randy was after his physical death. Randy was courageous and lived his life with honor. He was a hero!

I already had 11 years in the law enforcement profession by this time and had seen my share of death and trauma. I continued to carry on like nothing was wrong. But the violent, on-duty death of a fellow officer was just horrific, and I can't even begin to describe how it feels unless you've been in a similar position. I even briefly considered getting out of police work. But, if I went another 19 years, I could retire and receive a good pension. *Besides, if you fall off a horse, you must get back on that horse and continue riding it,* I thought. So I returned to work and had to drive by the location of the shooting every day on my way into the station. I got a nervous feeling every time I drove by it. My heart was still broken, and I became an overly protective rooster when it came to the well-being of my deputies. But my BCSO days were soon coming to an end, and I put the house up for sale.

Working for the Butte County Sheriff's Department was an honor and a blessing. It really molded me into the kind of cop I was going to be for the last 19 years of my career. I became an FTO, made the hostage negotiation team, worked a specialized detail in Chapmantown, was promoted to sergeant, and was the K-9 Team supervisor. I am very grateful for the time I spent there. But sadly, my time ended due to divorce and the fact I wanted to be geographically closer to my daughters.

Overview of shooting scene, May 21, 1997.

In honor of hero deputy sheriff, Randy Jennings
(January 22, 1959 – May 21, 1997).

Chapter 12

San Jacinto

I started working for the San Jacinto Police Department in July of 1997. I traded in my khaki over dark green uniform for midnight blues. I was once again a city cop, and my first assignment was as a patrol field supervisor and a watch commander on the night shift. The divorce was final, and I could be free to seek female companionship if I wanted to. My house in Oroville sold a few months into my job change, and I was finally free from having to pay the mortgage on top of the rent I paid for the house I rented in San Jacinto. I got to spend time with my daughters, and my ex, Kaleigh, and I were able to work out a schedule that worked for both of us and the girls. This was a new start for me, especially after the shooting in which my friend was killed. However, I still didn't fully and completely process what had happened. I just immersed myself in my new job and new surroundings. Little did I know I would become affected by another officer-involved shooting a year later.

Right around this time, I also enlisted in the California Army National Guard, which is part of the California State Military Department. I was wifeless, so there was nothing nor anybody to stop me from doing it. Later, I became an MP and senior personnel NCO at the battalion level. I was proud to have served my community, state, and nation as a part-time, traditional guardsman. I had known a couple of police officers who were guardsmen or army reservists that were deployed during the first Gulf War in 1991. I felt that I, too, had to do something for my nation's flag. However, I will keep my story limited to my time in law enforcement. I served faithfully in "the Guard" for almost six years but got out as weekend drills, annual training, and my full-time job as a police officer interfered with my custody time with my daughters. I have nothing but the utmost respect for today's active duty and reserve men and women.

I eventually met a lady named Laurie, who worked at San Jacinto City Hall, and we began to date. For the second time in my life, I found myself considering marriage. Yes, I worked kind of fast, but I enjoyed being in the company of a woman. I did not like being alone because I was not content with myself. I needed to hear the sound of someone else's voice in my empty house instead of listening to my own solitary thoughts. I learned I am not a very good bachelor because I do need the tender companionship of a lady. Laurie and I ended up getting married in August of 1999. We bought a lovely four-bedroom house and merged our children together to become a blended family. Her kids were older than mine as she had an 18-year-old daughter and a 15-year-old son. My Alexandra and Amanda were 7 and 4, respectively.

One evening while I was at work, I drove to the corporate yard to fuel up my patrol car. As I was standing next to the vehicle with the gas hose in hand, a gopher ran towards me and looked like it was either going to try and crawl up my pant legs or bite me. I shewed it off with my boot, but it came after me again. I took evasive action and tried to move out of its way. But everywhere I went, the gopher followed me. It seemed angry that I had chased it away in the first place, and it was going after me. What a sight to behold; an armed police officer being chased around the parking lot by a little gopher. Finally, I gave it a good punt with my boot, and it flew off into the distance, landed, and ran the other way. Maybe it had rabies because it was acting so aggressive; I just don't know. But in retrospect, it made me laugh.

I really grew professionally during my career at SJPD. One of my collateral assignments was as the department's K-9 sergeant like I was in Butte County. I also became the department coordinator for the police explorer and FTO programs. Yes, things were pretty good, and I cut back on my drinking as life seemed to be going along just dandy. I enjoyed my job immensely and was involved in a lot of crazy, dangerous, and fast-paced events. I loved being in the field with my officers and going on calls with them. If there was a shooting, I was there. If there was a bank robbery, I was there. I responded on all high-priority calls with my team whenever I could.

One cool winter day in December of 1998, while working as the dayshift watch commander, the alert tone came over the radio, which got my attention. The dispatcher broadcasted a call of a major injury traffic collision on Sanderson Avenue south of Ramona Expressway. It didn't sound good as more reports of the crash came flooding into the dispatch center. I responded to the crash site along with a couple of my officers. When I arrived, I could see that it was a head-on collision involving a small sedan and a pickup truck. The driver of the pickup truck, who had caused the crash by going over the double yellow traffic separation lines, was conscious and speaking.

Officer Hill and I began to tend to the needs of the victims in the sedan. The driver was a man in his late 30s or early 40s, and the passenger in the right front seat was a woman in her late 30s. The woman exited the car without too much assistance and began screaming for her baby. I didn't see a baby until I looked in the backseat of the mangled wreck and saw the car seat containing the lifeless body of an infant girl.

Officer Hill and I asked the driver some preliminary triage questions until the fire department, and paramedics arrived. He was conscious but seemed to be fading. He kept telling us, "Don't let her see me, don't let her see me." He didn't want his female passenger, who was also his fiancé, to see him in such rough shape. He had to be cut out and extricated from the vehicle. A ground ambulance would not have made it quickly enough, so the man was loaded onto an air ambulance helicopter that had landed in an adjacent field. As he was being loaded into the aircraft, he said, "take my wallet." Officer Hill reached into the man's pants pocket and took out his wallet. After opening the wallet and glancing at the contents, Officer Hill handed me the wallet. I took a look and saw the police officer badge from a neighboring agency inside.

One of the flight crew said loudly, "He crashed, and they began to conduct CPR on the man." The helicopter had not taken off yet, and the crew worked CPR on the man for a good 10 to 15 minutes until they pronounced him dead. My heart sank, and I now had the job of making notification to his department that their officer was deceased. It was one of the many calls I had made during my career that I will always remember. Officer Hill notified the female passenger that not only her baby didn't make it but that her fiancé had died on board the helicopter.

That one stayed with me for a while. Finally, I finished my day shift and went home at the end of the day. When I was finally relaxed and sitting on my couch in the comfort of my living room, I began to weep uncontrollably. Laurie did not know how to react as this was the first time in our five months of marriage that she had seen me this way. I had a glass of wine, cried it out, and went to sleep. The following day I got out of bed, showered, and prepared for work as if nothing had happened. I got pretty good at suppressing all of the trauma and grief I had seen.

It was July 2001, and Laurie and I were going to go on vacation back east. I was excited to take some time off from work and see a part of the country that I had never been to before. My phone rang on July 27th, and it was Jim Norman from the Butte County Sheriff's Department. I was elated to hear Jim's voice, but I could tell that something was wrong. Jim told me, "Larry Estes was shot and killed at work last night." "No," I exclaimed! "What happened?" Jim said that Larry was on his way home in his unmarked sheriff's vehicle when another deputy, Bill Hunter, had requested a backup unit to go make contact with a burglary suspect who had broken into a house and stole some items, including several firearms.

Deputy Hunter was a newer deputy, and I did not know him. He was only 26- years old. Jim went on to say that Bill Hunter and Larry Estes arrived at the suspect's house and made entry into the house. Although Deputy Hunter and Lieutenant Estes had their pistols drawn when they went inside, their entrance into the small cabin was met with immediate gunfire, and Deputy Hunter was shot in the head. Larry Estes engaged the suspect, and a hellacious gun battle ensued. There were over two-dozen rounds exchanged in the gunfight. Larry was hit four times and died on the scene. The suspect was also struck, and he later died.

I was struck with grief upon hearing the news. When Laurie got home from work, I told her that we were canceling our vacation plans to attend a funeral. The following week, I went up to Chico, CA, for the joint memorial service for Deputy Hunter and Lieutenant Larry Estes. I saw all of the people I used to work with, which was great, but the circumstances in which we were reunited were tragic. It drummed up all of my memories of Randy Jennings's death only four years earlier. I drove in the funeral procession in a marked San Jacinto Police car. The procession went past my old patrol area, Chapmantown, and the streets were lined with people paying their respects. As we passed by, I saw several people from the neighborhood who I recognized. They were waving American flags, and some were saluting. I lost it as tears began welling up in my eyes.

When I returned home from northern California, I found out I was getting reassigned from being a patrol watch commander to the position of detective sergeant. We only had five general detectives and a narcotics detective assigned to the investigations bureau. But I was elated; what a great opportunity! This meant I would be turning in my marked patrol car for an unmarked police vehicle and trading my uniform for plain clothes.

San Jacinto is a city of about 45,000 residents and used to be kind of a retirement community back in the 70s and 80s. But it had turned into a commuter town where people drove to other parts of the county to work. There was a significant gang, parolee, and drug problem in San Jacinto. So, it was needless to say I stayed pretty busy in my new position. I got called out to homicide scenes at all times of the day and night and was also charged with the responsibility of investigating a few officer-involved shootings. The work was interesting and exciting at times.

I continued to promote, and eventually, in May 2002, I was promoted to the rank of commander. The rank was the number two position in the department, immediately below the chief of police. I served as second in command and managed the department's daily operations. Ironically, I already had a three-week vacation scheduled which started about one week after my promotion. Laurie and I went on a long and relaxing trip. I was notified when I was away that another homicide in the city happened in a downtown bar. But, life went on as usual.

On the night after I got back from vacation, I was sound asleep when my phone rang around 3:00 am. A graveyard shift dispatcher told me that "Officer Babcock had just been shot." As I tried to comprehend what she had just told me, I said, "What?" She again told me that Officer Everett Babcock had just been shot but that his wound was not fatal. She further explained there was an exchange of gunfire between Everett and the suspect and that the suspect was still out on foot somewhere in a neighborhood. That was something no cop wanted to hear, although I was thankful Everett would survive his wounds. I suited up, got in my unmarked Crown Victoria, and drove to the scene. I had been the commander for all of four weeks, three of which were spent away from home on vacation, and now this happened. When I arrived at the scene, there were already marked police units from Hemet PD, the Riverside County Sheriff's Department, and San Jacinto PD present.

To make a long story shorter, a multi-agency team of officers and I ended up tracking the shooting suspect to a ghetto area called "the shoe" in the City of Moreno Valley a few days afterward. A "snitch" had told us where to find him and pinpointed the apartment where the suspect was holed up. We went to the Moreno Valley Police Station, which is a Riverside County Sheriff's Department contract policing agency, and linked up with their special enforcement team. We conducted an operational briefing and then headed out to the shoe. I took up a position on the perimeter while the entry team hit the apartment's front door. The suspect was located hiding up in the attic. He refused to come down, so a sheriff's canine was sent into the crawl space, where he subsequently got hold of the suspect and bit him. This was the incentive the suspect needed in order to comply and come out of the attic. The suspect had a gunshot wound to one of his ankles. So we knew that one of Everett's rounds had hit the bad guy during the exchange of gunfire.

I learned a few things during my time as commander at SJPD. One of those key points is that I couldn't make everybody happy all of the time. Along with more responsibility comes making some unpopular decisions. At the first-line level, officers are typically sheltered and filtered from the confusion of politics. But as they rise through the chain of command, politics becomes an unpleasant reality as a part of the job. It is truly an art to be able to balance the will of elected officials with the realities of police work. Even city councilmen and women think they are experts in policing, which they are not. My heart truly belonged to the police profession and the men and women who performed the job. I was never any good with the political aspect of executive-level management.

We had several bank robberies involving a suspect who dressed as a mail carrier. His method of operation was to walk into a bank in a US Postal Service uniform, point a pistol at the teller, and demand he or she put money in his mailbag. He'd then walk out the door and lay low until his next robbery. We nicknamed him the Postal Bandit. He was wanted for multiple bank robberies in Los Angeles, Riverside, and San Bernardino Counties.

One day while sitting in my office, I heard a radio call of a silent bank robbery alarm at a local financial institution being broadcast. Within less than a minute, the dispatcher chimed in with an update stating that a bank employee had called 911 and stated that the silent alarm was actually a robbery that had just occurred. The Postal Bandit had struck again! This time a sharp bank manager was able to get a vehicle description and partial license number of the getaway car.

I walked out to the backlot at the station and got in my unmarked car. I decided to head towards the bank driving a parallel street while marked units were responding to the actual crime scene. As I was traveling east on Seventh Street approaching Hewitt Street, I saw a car matching the suspect vehicle description going the opposite direction on westbound Seventh Street. I turned my car around and got in behind it. As I did so, I could see that the license number matched the partial license number that the caller provided. I told dispatch I was behind the vehicle and waited for marked units to join me so that we could make a high-risk traffic stop. Within a couple of minutes, we made the stop and took the Postal Bandit into custody. A very realistic-looking plastic replica pistol was recovered from the vehicle that he used to commit the robberies. It felt good to get him off of the streets and to help some of the other agencies clear their bank robbery cases.

In late 2003, my chief resigned from his position at SJPD. He said he and the city manager had philosophical differences, and he couldn't work for him anymore. The chief that left was my mentor and friend, and I was still learning the intricate details of my position as commander. What was I going to do now? I ended up becoming the acting chief for a short time and felt like the weight of the world was on my shoulders. I had to have regular interactions with the city council and the city manager. After hours phone calls from council members became regular and routine for me.

Suddenly, I was thrown into having to write staff reports for the city manager and council members and complete the department's budget. I had to terminate a probationary police officer who was dishonest and already had an inappropriate relationship with a woman he had met on the job. I found myself going to work between 5:00 and 6:00 am to get a jump start on my workdays, and my stress level went up with my new responsibilities. There was no more mentoring for me anymore by anyone, but instead *winging it* and just trying to make the best decisions that I could at the time. Some people say it's lonely at the top, and I felt like the one-man-band.

One day near the end of 2003, I attended a meeting of law enforcement administrators from all over the county. During a break at the meeting, one of the assistant sheriffs (the rank below undersheriff) from the Riverside County Sheriff's Department (RSD) told me that my city manager had been talking to members of the sheriff's administration about contracting with the county to provide law enforcement services to the City of San Jacinto. He said that he just thought I should know as he didn't want me to get blindsided by the news at the last minute. I couldn't believe it. But it was a trend at that time for municipalities to contract with the Sheriff because it was more cost-effective. 15 or 16 cities in the county were already contracting with RSD for police services.

I contacted one of the city council members that I knew and trusted reasonably well at the day's end. I confronted him with the news that I had heard earlier in the day, and he didn't deny it. He told me that the San Jacinto Police Officer's Association (POA) was fighting it out with the City during labor negotiations. The POA wanted better retirement benefits, and the City could not afford it. It was a source of contention between both factions. So the city decided to start looking at contracting with RSD.

I knew that the department head or "top brass" in city police departments that are taken over by RSD usually found themselves out of a job. I was 39 years old and still had 11 years to go until I was eligible for retirement. What should I do; try to find another job or stick it out and take my chances with the Sheriff? I decided to stick it out in the hope I could secure a position with RSD. However, I felt like the captain of a sinking ship during my last few months in the department. It turns out I had to negotiate for a position with the Undersheriff and an assistant sheriff. They told me I would more than likely be hired as a sergeant with RSD. Even though it was a demotion for me, I was just happy I was still going to have a job. Being a sergeant is one of the best jobs in any department.

San Jacinto Police Sgt. Keith Knotek, Huntington Beach Police Sgt. "JB" Hume and Huntington Beach Police Officer Erik Himert, at the 1998 California Peace Officer Memorial ceremony, Sacramento, California.

San Jacinto Police Commander Keith Knotek presenting outgoing police chief Stuart Heller with a Meritorious Service Award, 2003.

In honor of hero Butte County Sheriff's Lieutenant Larry Estes (June 10, 1940 – July 24, 2001).

Chapter 13

Riverside County

My first day at RSD was May 1, 2004. Only about 1/4th of us were hired by the Sheriff, and the rest of the officers either found jobs at different departments or ended up unemployed. Riverside County Sheriff's Department is the third-largest sheriff's agency out of all 58 counties in the State of California. My first assignment was as a shift supervisor at the Robert Presley Detention Center (RPDC) in downtown Riverside. I wasn't happy at all about that because I was previously told I would be left in San Jacinto to help with the transition. I learned later that the Sheriff did not want anyone from the old SJPD administration at the new sheriff's contract city. That actually made sense once it was explained to me.

I spent three years at RPDC and went through my second divorce after I turned 40 years old. Laurie was having an affair with a coworker, and she broke the news to me on Father's Day 2005. We separated and went through the divorce process. Just like during my first divorce, I began dropping weight like crazy. My uniform looked like a sack hanging on my body as I lost about 20 pounds. I eventually did the online dating thing but became very disillusioned with it. My alcohol consumption got worse as I began to use booze as a relaxant again.

Earlier in this book, I mentioned a friend named Randy that was in the police explorer program with me, not to be confused with Deputy Randy Jennings, who was killed in the line of duty in Butte County. My childhood friend Randy Williams and I were close and remained "thick as thieves" into adulthood. Randy got married to his wife at a young age and had a son. They moved from Orange County to Fresno

County in the late 90s. Randy worked as a public safety officer at Fresno Pacific University.

Randy and his wife fell on hard times in their marriage and were going through a divorce. Randy still loved his wife and did not want to see the demise of his own marriage. But his estranged wife was adamant about living her life separate from Randy. So in October of 2006, Randy decided he wanted to start over and reinvent himself by moving back to southern California. He applied for a position in my department as a correctional deputy and came down from Fresno to go through the testing process.

Randy stayed overnight at my house in the evening before his physical agility test and written exam. Since I had to work a graveyard shift that night, I left Randy a spare house key so that he could come and go as he pleased. He drove to downtown Riverside that evening and joined some of my coworkers and me for dinner. Randy seemed excited and optimistic about his physical agility exam scheduled for the following morning and a written test. Randy drove back to my house around 10:00 pm so that he could get a good night's sleep.

I left work with my carpool partner at 6:00 am the following morning. When I got home, I expected to see Randy up and getting ready to go to the sheriff's academy for his tests. But the house was silent and dark. I believe the testing process started at 8:00 am, and Randy was still in bed at 6:45 am. Maybe he overslept, I thought. So I knocked on my guest bedroom door and said, "Randy, you need to get up." But there was no acknowledgment. Perhaps he didn't hear me, so I opened the bedroom door and called out to him in a louder tone. But there was still silence in the room, so I went inside.

At that point, I saw Randy's body lying face down on the bed and a little bit of blood on his pillow.

"No," I exclaimed! I know what a dead body looks like because I've seen plenty of them in my lifetime. Although I noticed that post-mortem lividity (settling of the blood) had already set in his body, I still had to check Randy for a pulse just to be sure. "Oh, my God, why?" My friend was dead at the age of 42. This was so unexpected. I started thinking to myself, was this suicide; did he ingest some type of chemical or overdose on something? I called 911, and a deputy from the San Jacinto Sheriff's Station came to the house along with paramedics. The deputy asked me a series of questions and suggested that I'd be the one to make the death notification to Randy's next of kin.

I found Randy's cell phone on the nightstand next to his bed and located his parent's phone number in his list of contacts. I called and woke both of them up from a sound sleep. As one can imagine, their reaction to what I had just told them was very passionate and emotional. This was the last thing I had expected when Randy came down to visit me. The most bizarre thing about the whole situation was that around midnight while I was still at work, I suddenly had a strange feeling that Randy had passed away. I can't explain it as I've never experienced anything like it before, nor have I since that time. It turns out the coroner's office deemed Randy's cause of death to be a massive coronary event. I felt empty inside, but life went on.

I met my third and current wife, Lilia ("Lily"), at the jail in 2007. She worked for Riverside County Superior Court as a pretrial services investigator and was assigned to RPDC. We began to date, and I fell hard and fast for Lily. When people ask Lily and me how we met, we tell them, "We met in jail."

Lily and I were eventually married in May 2008. For me, the third time really is the charm. Lily really helps to center me, and we complement each other emotionally in so many ways. God has blessed me with a true partner in life, and I am so grateful for her.

In June 2007, I was transferred from RPDC to the Patrol Operations Division at the Southwest Station, located near Temecula, CA. I was finally getting to be back out in the field and driving a black & white once again. I hadn't worked patrol since I was promoted to detective sergeant at SJPD in 2001. I may have been a little bit rusty, but I soon learned how to do things "the RSD way." Lily and I bought a new house in Murrieta, and my commute to work was only about a five-minute drive. I worked on a couple of different assignments, and life could not have been any better. Lily and I went to church, but I still had no real relationship with God.

During my time at Southwest Station, I experienced more death, grief, trauma, shootings, stabbings, and other various critical incidents. I won't go into detail about many of those incidents out of respect to the decedents' surviving family members. The stress started getting to me, and my PTS started flaring up again. I was not sleeping, and I started having bad "cop dreams" or nightmares. In 2009, I started self-medicating with wine. I drank about half a bottle of wine every night before bed so that I could fall asleep. I did this until around 2010, when the wine started wearing off and becoming ineffective. I switched to hard liquor and would use it to "knock myself out" before bedtime.

I'll never forget going on a call in the wee hours of the morning, which really affected me. I was the closest unit when an unknown trouble call came out over the radio. The dispatcher advised that a 14-year-old boy had called to report that he was awakened by two loud banging sounds. When he went to his parent's bedroom, he found both of them unresponsive on the floor. I had a delayed response time because it was a very foggy morning, and there were a lot of morning commuters on the roadway that were heading into work. My backup unit was coming from a long distance away.

When I arrived on the residential street where the house was located, I saw the caller standing in front of the house to wave me down. I found the boy's 12-year-old brother standing in the living room as I entered the house. The boys told me their parent's bedroom was the first room on the left on the second floor and that there was nobody else inside the house. I told the boys to wait on their front porch while I cautiously went up the stairs with my pistol drawn. As I reached the bedroom, I saw a woman's body kneeling next to the bed. Her knees were on the ground, and her head was resting on the bed in a puddle of blood. There was a pillow on the ground, and there were feathers all around. I deduced that she was shot in the back of the head and that the shooter put a pillow to the back of her head to muffle the sound of the gunshot.

Then I noticed the body of a naked male on the floor near the foot of the bed. His head was also lying in a puddle of blood, and there was a Model 1911-style pistol on the floor next to the body with the hammer cocked back. Based on what I had seen, I figured that the husband had shot his wife and then himself. The eldest son heard the shots and was awakened by the gunshots. He got out of bed and found the bodies. What a tragedy. I advised dispatch to contact our Central Homicide Unit and called for additional units to assist with containing the perimeter of the crime scene.

When I came downstairs and asked the boys to come back inside the living room, I broke the news to them that their parents had passed away. The 12-year-old boy started crying alligator tears, and it truly broke my heart. I told him that I wished I could do or say something to make everything better, and he replied, "Me too." I felt so helpless. The older brother appeared to be in shock. There was nothing I could do except be sympathetic and comforting while I waited for the additional units to arrive. At that time, my daughters were both the same age as those boys. I've been to other murder suicides, but this one really sucker-punched me in the gut. I just filed it away in the back of my mind like all of the other horrible stuff I had experienced.

In 2010, Lily was diagnosed with a serious health issue, and my mom passed away due to complications of Alzheimer's disease. I was stressing out inside, but I held it back and kept it all inside. In 2011, I was involved in another critical incident that pushed me over the edge. My drinking got even worse as I started drinking copious amounts of alcohol on my days off from work. As I was doing it, I knew it was bad, but I thought I could stop myself at any time. I did not drink on workdays except for a few shots of hard liquor before going to bed. I never showed up to work under the influence or with alcohol on my breath. But I was coming apart at the seams. I had to do something and had to do it fast! This self-medicating with alcohol had to stop.

One afternoon, I built up the courage to tell my supervisor that I had a drinking problem and that I thought I had PTS because I was experiencing the symptoms of it. I felt so vulnerable because this was not something that cops did. It was a sign of weakness, I thought. My boss gave me some information on employee psychological assistance and filled out worker's compensation on my behalf because my alcoholism and PTS were directly related to my job as a peace officer. My lieutenant told me that he commended me for my courage to come forward and admit that I had a problem.

I began to see a county contract psychologist who seemed to help for a while. But the worker's compensation benefits only paid for seven visits. So after my counseling visits ended, I continued to go to work, "white-knuckling" it and staying sober. Lily was happy that I stopped drinking, and things seemed to be getting a little bit better. I was feeling pretty good about work and life in general. I was a little over three years away from retirement and was beginning to see the light at the end of the tunnel. For me, the goal was to make it to that milestone called retirement with no more trauma or drama.

I was working as the swing shift watch commander out of Southwest Station one evening and decided to go home and have some dinner. I lived within our station's patrol area, which was very convenient for a lot of reasons. It was a really busy shift, and most of my guys and gals were tied up on calls for service. So, I listened to my police radio as I started to take my first few bites of food. I started telling Lily about my day when the radio crackled with a report of a man brandishing a gun in a residential neighborhood. One of the deputies had to clear from a call he was already on in order to respond to this higher priority call. I told the dispatcher I would be en route as a backup unit since no one else was available. Plus, I was only about 10 minutes away from where the incident was occurring. I left Lily and my dinner on the table. I told her I would hopefully be back home shortly.

As I arrived on the street where the brandishing had occurred, I was waved down by the caller. The man who was standing next to a pickup truck that was parked alongside the curb appeared to be frazzled. He told me that he had stopped in front of a house to write some notes down as he spoke on the cell phone with his boss when the agitated resident of the house came outside holding a pistol in his hand. The man, in this case, the suspect, approached the caller, yelling profanities and questioning why the man was parked in front of his house. When the man explained that he was just parked so he could talk on his phone, the "gunslinger" pointed the pistol at him and told him to leave. The caller said the man appeared to be drunk or under the influence of something.

Another unit arrived, and it was Deputy Dan Thompson. At that point, we had probable cause to arrest the individual for assault with a deadly weapon (firearm). In California, it is a felony to point a gun at someone in a threatening manner even without firing a shot. I told Dan what the caller had explained to me, and we went to the suspect's house to make contact and more than likely arrest him. Dan banged on the front door multiple times, announcing to the man inside that we were with the sheriff's department and to come to the door. We did this multiple times without success. Dan went to the front corner of the house on the porch to see the door. I took up a position behind a large pillar or support post located in front and adjacent to the door. Dan and I waited silently to see what the suspect would do next.

I saw movement in the front window as the man peeked through the curtains. I do not think he saw me, and I know he didn't see Dan. Then the front door opened slowly. The only thing I saw was a right arm coming through the front door with a pistol clenched in hand. I already had my sidearm out and at the ready. I placed my front site on what would have been the center of mass as soon as he stepped outside, and I felt the pressure of my right index finger being applied to the trigger on my pistol. Fortunately for the suspect, the barrel of his gun was pointed straight out at the front yard, and I was off to the side. Had the barrel swung in my direction, the outcome would have been different, and Dan and I would have been the ones walking away unharmed since we had the tactical advantage.

Dan and I shouted for the man to drop the gun about five times before he finally did so. We were able to get him "proned-out" on the front porch, where we took him into custody without further incident. The suspect was all hopped up on prescription medication and was completely out of his mind at the time. Another deputy showed up to take the report, Dan transported the suspect to jail, and I ended up driving back to my house to finish my dinner. When I arrived home, Lily asked me how everything went on the call I had just been on. I told her I almost just shot someone but that everything had turned out just fine. I finished my meal, kissed Lily goodbye, and then headed back out onto the streets. Think about that; it is not normal to come so close to nearly taking a human life and then eating dinner right afterward like nothing even happened. However, this is a common reality in the world of law enforcement. This is just one of many incidents like this that happened during my career.

In October of 2011, my PTS started flaring up due to some traumatic work-related events with which I had a hard time coping. On October 20, I met my friend at a bar after a fraternal organization meeting we had attended together. On the way home, I stopped at a liquor store and bought a bottle of hard liquor for my drive home. I thought it would take the edge off by the time I got home, and I would just go to sleep when I got there. I was driving hammered on the northbound I-15 Freeway and was subsequently stopped by the California Highway Patrol. I was a peace officer and logically knew better not to do what I was doing. But the alcoholic mind does not reason well or make the best decisions when under stress. Think again for those of you who think that police officers have a "get out of jail free card" for the mere fact that they carry a badge. I was arrested for misdemeanor DUI and booked into jail. I was so humiliated, embarrassed, and extremely ashamed. The sad part about the whole ordeal was that it was of my own doing. In retrospect, most of my lousy life decisions involved alcohol.

I suffered consequences at work and home because of my actions. Everybody at Southwest Station heard about my arrest. *How would I be received when I return to work*, I thought? On my first day back to work after the arrest, I talked to my patrol personnel during the afternoon briefing about what had happened. I was very open and transparent about what had occurred and my part in it. Some deputies appreciated my candor, and others thought I was a piece of trash for breaking the law. We, as police officers, are very hard on each other. I, too, used to be highly critical of others.

I tried to rely on my own human understanding to stay sober because I was the one in control of my destiny. Even though my best thinking at the time landed me in jail, I thought I would only drink a little bit to take the edge off. I requested a transfer out of patrol to a less stressful assignment. I knew I couldn't remain out in the field and keep my head in the game when things got stressful. I was tired of seeing all of the death and human destruction I experienced out on the streets. I never wanted to see another dead body again for as long as I lived. I submitted a transfer request to leave the Field Operations Division and go to either the Court Services or Corrections Division.

I found out my transfer request was approved and that I'd be getting sent to one of the jail facilities. I also learned my fate and found out I would not be terminated and kept my rank. However, I received an 80 reduction in pay as my departmental discipline, so it hit me in the pocketbook. I plead guilty to the DUI and received informal probation. After I tied up those loose ends, I went on leave for 30 days. Lily and I took the time to go on a road trip vacation for a couple of weeks while I was off work. The time away from the stressors of the job did me some good, and spending time with Lily was a blessing.

During my last three years on the job before retirement, I was a jail facility's transportation unit supervisor. It actually ended up being a really great assignment. During that time, I was able to go back to school and earn my Bachelor's Degree. I worked regular hours and had weekends off from work. I had the freedom to go on transportation runs throughout the state with my deputies and really enjoyed my team. I could feel my stress level go down, but I was still drinking, only not as much as I used to drink. I did not want to become the kind of retired guy who sits on the couch, watches TV, and drinks all day.

We sold our house in Murrieta near the end of my career and purchased a home in Prescott Valley, Arizona. Lily and I would move to Arizona after my 50th birthday and upon my retirement. Things were going well, and I decided I was going to stay sober and not drink anymore about six months prior to retirement. Finally, the day came in January of 2015 when I retired after 30 years in law enforcement. Lily and I made the move to Prescott and life became sweeter.

Riverside County Sheriff's Southwest Division
patrol days, 2008.

Lily and Keith's wedding day, May 2008.

Goodbye, California, January 2015.

Chapter 14

Post-retirement

Lily started getting bored after retirement, and I'll admit that I did too. I started an online Master's Degree program and went to work for the State of Arizona for a short time. Lily started working at the magistrate court in the town in which we lived. After only four months, I ended my job with the State because I was commuting 91 miles each way every day. The drive was getting to me, and I didn't really have to work. After I left my job, I began to immerse myself in various volunteer organizations. Although I received no monetary compensation for volunteering, it felt good to give back to the community.

I managed to stay sober for more than a year and didn't drink any alcoholic beverages. Then one afternoon in 2017, I heard some terrible news. One of the deputies from my former agency had a wife who had just returned to work at the Palm Springs Police Department after being on maternity leave. She went on a domestic dispute between a family and their son and was shot and killed in the line of duty along with another Palm Springs police officer. All of my past seemed to have collided with the present, and I envisioned gunfire, muzzle flash, and fear in my mind once again. It shook me to my core, and I went out and bought a bottle of rum. I came home and secretly drank again that day which Lily naturally discovered.

I became enraged when Lily called me out on my uncontrolled drinking. I yelled and turned into a completely different person when I drank. We've all heard of the Doctor Jekyll and Mr. Hyde personality, and that was me; just add alcohol. Lily was heartbroken, and I went on to drink off and on again for a few more months. My drinking was out of control, and so was my demeanor. I lost my inhibitions when I drank, and I started acting out on my ungodly desires. I ruined friendships because of my drinking and my reckless behavior. I said incredibly hurtful things to friends and loved ones, and they were finally getting sick of it. My impairment caused me to make bad decisions and to do and say things I normally would never think of doing. I did not like where my life was headed if I was to keep drinking. I caused extreme wreckage in the past and didn't want to go that route anymore. Life was generally pretty good as long as I abstained from drinking alcohol.

I had to do something. I admitted to myself that I was an alcoholic and that my life had become unmanageable because of my abuse of alcoholic beverages. I started going to Alcoholics Anonymous meetings and built up some sobriety time. Lily told me she was proud of me and thankful for my efforts to get better. Once again, I was on a plateau, and things were looking up. I was feeling good about life in general and was losing the weight that I had put on from drinking alcohol. However, I still had not given my entire life over to God and did not connect with Him daily in prayer like I should have been doing. After retirement, I did an online undergraduate certificate program in advanced biblical studies through Liberty University. So, I improved my theological and Biblical knowledge but still had no sustained and deep spiritual connection with God. I wanted a genuine relationship with God, one that I could see and feel in my soul. But I didn't know how to garner and maintain such a relationship. Little did I know that it would take another significant emotional event two years later to reach that point finally.

Lily and I got dialed into a local church in Prescott, Arizona, and began attending Sunday services. The church had an abundance of different programs and a lot going on. I liked best that the senior minister, Pastor Jack, was a recovering drug addict and alcoholic. It had been decades since he had struggled with his addictions. But he spoke freely, candidly, and transparently about his dark past and his redemption through Christ Jesus. The pastor talked a lot about God's healing power, redemption, mercy, and grace. Now, this is a man I could relate to!

My days were filled with volunteering for the various organizations I belonged to, studying, researching, and writing papers for my Master's program. I eventually received my Master of Arts in Organizational Leadership in April 2017. I became interested in my ancestral line and genealogy because of my bloodline lineage to some of the first American patriots and to British royalty. I joined several hereditary societies and started doing things with those fraternal organizations. I was being productive, staying busy, and doing good things. However, my prayer life was still lacking, and my daily connection with God was weak. All of the volunteering in the world and good works weren't going to fill my spiritual void.

Because I believed in God and recognized His sacrifice by sending Jesus to die a painful death on a cross, I wanted to honor and serve Him in some capacity. Granted, I still had no daily connection or relationship with God, but I was acutely aware that he remained God and king supreme. So, I got appointed as a chaplain with an organization I belonged to at the time in order to respond to crises on a "care team" if it was needed. Even though I was still selfish, I wanted to help my fellow men and women in a different kind of capacity rather than showing up on a scene with a pistol and looking for a threat.

Later in 2017, I started teaching part-time at a local university. I enjoyed the work and was glad to have something else meaningful to do in retirement. The extra income didn't hurt either, especially when it came to paying for our post-retirement private medical insurance. Being in front of a classroom full of students continued to feed my ego and my desire to be the center of attention. However, the hour-long commute and time spent teaching kept me away from AA meetings and from fellowship with my sponsor Steve, who had volunteered to guide me through the program. I was learning a lot about sobriety and how to stay sober, but I got "too busy" to practice the program every day. Alcohol is tricky that way, but it takes whatever it takes to completely surrender your life over to the care of God. Some people get it right away and others, like me, have to be completely broken to the brink of destruction in order to begin the road to recovery, the pathway to a new and beautiful life. It's never too late to start over.

Chapter 15

The Beginning of the End

In the summer of 2017, I found out that my dear friend and mentor, JB Hume, was diagnosed with colon cancer which had spread to other organs. His prognosis was not good. But, I took to prayer and uplifted his situation to God every day. On Thanksgiving Day 2017, I received word that JB had passed away from his disease. I was devastated. JB was only eight years older than me and should have lived a long and vibrant life. In my mind, I questioned why God would allow this to happen to such a loving and caring man. But I managed to stay sober through it all.

My dad had been living in Wildomar, CA, for several decades and his health was failing. Lily and I were kind of hoping we could bring him out to Arizona to live with us, but he decided to get married again. That in itself is an entirely different story that I won't go into at this time. On April 15, 2018, my sister Cindy called me and told me that my dad had a heart attack and was in the hospital in Murrieta. I told Cindy and Lily that I was going to leave for California the following morning to see my dad. I headed out early that Monday morning and began to make the five-hour drive to Murrieta.

During my drive, my dad called me and tried to talk me out of going to see him. He tried to downplay his condition and said that he was fine. I told him that he had just had a heart attack, so he wasn't fine, and nothing could stop me from seeing him. I arrived at the hospital, and my sister and her husband were in the room with my father. I spoke with the doctor, who informed me that since my dad was 87 years old, he had already had five-way bypass surgery in 2008 and was in a frail condition that the only thing they could do was release him to home hospice care and make him comfortable.

When we are young, we think our parents, loved ones, and ourselves will live forever. I had already lost my mom in 2010, and now it appeared as if I was going to lose my father. On Wednesday, April 18, 2018, my dad was released from the hospital and sent home. My sister and I sat with dad and took care of him for several days. Early on Friday morning, I received a call from my dad's wife. She told me my dad was not doing well and that she was having a hard time getting him out of bed. I called Lily, who was still in Arizona, and told her she needed to take time off from work and drive out to California to be with us, which she did.

Lily arrived at my dad's house, and we all spent time with him. In a very weak tone of voice, Dad said, "It's sure nice to have family here." About three hours after that statement, my dad passed away. My sister and I were now orphaned adults. I prayed to God and was stricken with grief. I did the funeral and memorial service planning and tried to hold it together. I felt empty inside and had a deep sense of loss. I had no more living parent, grandparents, and many of my aunts and uncles had died too. All of my family histories seemed to have died along with my loved ones. I stayed in California for almost two weeks and finally returned home.

My dad and I used to talk on the phone every Sunday. I found myself wanting to call dad on Sundays for several months after he had passed away. It was just something that I had grown accustomed to, but the stark reality set in that he was no longer around to talk to. I wished that I could ask my dad questions about our family history and about his childhood days. He'd tell us tales from his past when he was still alive. Although I remembered most of them, there were still more questions I had wanted to ask him.

Life went on as usual. I continued to do my volunteer work in the Civil Air Patrol, which gave me purpose and kept me flying with the aircrew. In June 2018, I was at Kirtland Air Force Base in Albuquerque, NM, for a nine-day training course for Civil Air Patrol. When I was away, a close family friend called me and told me that her mother had died. Wow, only two months after my dad had passed and a dear family friend had left this earthly world too.

In August 2018, Lily quit her job with the local court because she had begun drawing on her pension from her former employer in California. The following month my father-in-law became ill and was admitted to the hospital in Loma Linda, CA. The doctors could not give him a proper diagnosis because they couldn't figure out what was wrong with him. His condition was rapidly declining, and Lily had gone out to California to be with her mother and to keep vigil around her dad. He spent almost three months in the ICU and ultimately passed away on October 2, 2018. I could not believe that Lily and I had both lost our fathers within a six-month period. I had to love and support Lily, just as she was when my dad passed away. I grieved his death as if I was reliving my own father's death.

In February of 2019, my friend Eddie called me to tell me that his wife, Kelley, had unexpectedly passed away. I couldn't believe it. Kelley was younger than me. Eddie, Kelley, and I used to go to church youth groups together when we were kids. The two of them got married, and we have remained friends ever since that time. I had experienced four deaths of either family members or friends in just a short period of time. Everything from the past started colliding with the present time. I started dwelling on all of the deaths I had encountered over the years. I began to think about my own mortality and how long I had left. When close family and friends pass away so suddenly and in such a short period of time, it really does begin to affect one's mind in a negative way. At least it did in my particular case.

Two months later, I was notified by a friend that our mutual friend, Dan, had suddenly passed away, probably due to a heart attack. Dan was also one of my mentors along with JB in my early police explorer days. He was retired from law enforcement and active in his church's worship band. I couldn't believe it; Dan was gone too! Since I had no more professional life as a retired cop, I felt my personal life crashing down all around me. I fell into a deep depression after the news and decided to go visit my daughters, who were both living in northern Nevada at that time. Perhaps a visit with them would pull me out from the depths of sorrow.

Chapter 16

Broken

It is May 3, 2019, and I have recently lost my friend and mentor, Dan, to a massive heart attack. I am thinking about Dan as I am driving home to Prescott Valley, Arizona, after visiting my daughters who live in Northern Nevada. The loss of Dan weighs heavily on my mind. There is a half drank bottle of whiskey on my passenger seat, and I am speeding in the middle of the Nevada desert in an effort to get home quicker. Unfortunately, I had no knowledge that I was weaving all over the road. As I enter a small town where the speed limit drops down to 25 MPH, it is too late to react to the brake lights in front of me as the lead car slows down. As I slam on the breaks, my car is sent sliding into the back of the vehicle in front of me.

Three people are injured and are loaded into an air ambulance helicopter as I am placed in handcuffs and transported to jail for driving under the influence. This nightmare couldn't be happening. After all, I was a police officer at one time! My life has spiraled out of control. How did I get here? I squandered the life that I had at one time. I was facing possible prison time and possibly the loss of the rights I once had as a law-abiding citizen. I never thought I'd find myself in this position. I can't change what happened or what I had become at that moment. However, I could do something about the future, but only with God's grace and help.

As I spent four days in jail before being released, my heart and mind turned to God. Is this my rock bottom, I wonder? I cry out to God to heal the injured people and to help me deal with the aftermath of what I had done. I came to realize that I had become a horrible, deceitful, prideful, selfish, and reckless person. I finally fell on my knees in my jail cell and asked the God of Abraham to take away my pride, self-absorption, and my propensity for turning to alcohol when I am depressed. I needed His help because I was beyond being able to do anything humanly possible to recover from the path of destruction I had laid down without God in my life.

I remembered the program of Alcoholics Anonymous conveying that we alcoholics are all powerless over alcohol and that if we seek God's help, He could and would help us. I believed it with all of my heart as my best worldly thinking got me into bad situations. I was tired of ungodly, worldly thinking and wanted to live a quiet, drama-free, and God-pleasing life. The incomprehensible demoralization of being a slave to alcohol was the most helpless feeling I've ever had in my entire life. I began to spend time in meditation and prayer with my heavenly father every day from then forward.

Lily was ready to leave me. She had had enough of my bad, sinful, and dysfunctional behavior. She told me she was seriously considering moving back to California and leaving me in Arizona. My daughters were both hurt emotionally and upset by my actions. My entire family was worried about me, and it was uncertain what course I would take from that point forward. I was ruining the lives of my family and myself. I was distancing myself from my friends and the people I cared about. I had lost my moral compass and knew I could no longer continue that way. Only God's power, love, and mercy could restore my relationships with my family and make me whole. I humbly asked Him to do so, and soon the miracle began to take shape.

When we create or are handed a *shit sandwich,* we may have to eat it. I sure did. I had to make up for my past mistakes legally, civilly, and personally. It is one of those things we must do in order to chip away at the walls we build around ourselves with pride, ego, and not letting anyone inside for fear of revealing our true selves to another human being. The more we eat away at that sandwich, the more we are chipping away at the layers we must shed to become real and transparent. When we are honest, sincere, and transparent, we can make restitution and amends for our past bad choices. When we do so, it allows God to come in and begin rebuilding us.

Chapter 17

A New Beginning

I want to start this chapter off by saying that God loves us as we are. He wants to make us better if we surrender and allow Him to be the Lord of our lives. This is the part of my story where I actually started writing this book. After surrendering and putting my full trust in God, I woke up one morning about a week after the accident and felt different. I was focused and acutely aware of my sin and character defects. However, I felt a peace that I have never experienced before in a time of crisis. God made me fully aware of my deep-seated flaws, and I felt like, for the first time, I was compelled by the Holy Spirit to put my thoughts down on paper. Then I thought I would start from the beginning to constructively figure out how I arrived in this situation in the first place. God subsequently put it in my heart to share my story of strength, joy, and hope with anyone it might help. So, I began to write this book. I was finally broken, and God was starting to rebuild me into the man He always wanted me to be. The following few pages are the things God had revealed to me about myself and my sick spiritual condition.

I came to the realization that not only was I broken but that I had lived the majority of my adult life with the illusion that everything was fine. That was my answer to everything. How are you doing? "Great," I would answer. How was work, Keith? "Fine," I'd say. I put on a fake face every day in the hope that nobody else could see that everything was not fine. I did not want to burden anyone with my dark thoughts, and I absolutely did not want to become vulnerable by revealing the dark secrets and pain I held onto so fiercely. Some people actually call this condition depression. I didn't even really realize I was depressed and scared, as it was a feeling that just snuck up and consumed me.

I was living a lie as I was spiritually dead inside and was hurting from life events that I had let knock me down. I pointed my so-called righteous right finger at those who stumbled, struggled, and fell along life's highway instead of extending my right hand to pick them up and help them along the way. I came to the stark realization that I was not "all that and a bag of chips." I made "things, stuff," and people my happiness instead of the mere fact that God's gift of generous grace should be sufficient. I am not saying that every day is a picnic in the park when we walk in the full knowledge of God's love. No, there will be challenges; life happens! My point is that when we love, trust, and seek God's will, it makes those hurdles and bumps in the road easier to deal with.

I had to become broken in order to become teachable because my earthly human pride caused me to think I already knew everything. I was too smart for my own good. As I began to spend time in prayer and studying His word, God has been working in areas of my life that even I was fully unaware of until I hit my rock bottom. I was an extremely prideful, egotistical, self-important, and self-absorbed individual. Oh, how I was "so special" and looked down on others who I didn't believe rose to the level of my excellence. I was a Type-A person and couldn't just be a worker bee doing an admirable day's work. I had to be large and in charge, always in command of whatever I did. I needed people to recognize how wonderful I thought I really was.

As I looked back reflecting on my career, I came to realize that I wasn't some great law enforcement guru, supervisor, or manager. Although I genuinely loved and cared for the men and women I supervised, I was still self-centered. I tried to give the guys and gals support and the tools they needed to properly do their jobs. But my patrol team or specialized unit was my realm and reigned king supreme. I wish I had a chance to go back and have a do-over. But, since that is not possible I will continue to stay attuned to the Holy Spirit and try to keep doing the next right thing.

In fact, after I retired, I felt so highly of myself that I built a shrine room to myself with awards, plaques and various certificates to prove how great I was. Not too many people even venture into that inner sanctum part of our house. So if I didn't display all of the trappings of self-important pride for others to see, whom then? Maybe I hung up those token symbols to remind myself of my "glory days" and that I was and still am really awesome. Perhaps I did it to overcompensate for the emptiness I had felt inside. I have a friend named Steve who could see right through me. He had a saying, "You're just another bozo on the bus." I have another dear friend who told me that at one point, he had to take a break from spending time with me because I had become so arrogant. I felt embarrassed and ashamed. I never want to become that guy again.

Everything was about me. I discounted things that my wife brought to my attention because I wasn't ready to hear them. I took Lily and other family members for granted. There just wasn't enough room in our four-bedroom house, AND my big ego. In retrospect, I was a classic narcissist and became the very type of person I loathed during my law enforcement career. I used to make fun of self-centered people like me. I used to think that they were the ones with the problem, not me. Although there were little hints here and there about how prideful and self-centered I was – little hints that were just chipping away, I still didn't get it.

In law enforcement, anytime an enforcement stop is made of an individual, that person is required to obey any lawful order the officer may give them. We had a saying in the profession that when we were dealing with a problematic individual on some type of contact, it went like this, "Ask you, tell you, make you." This really meant that the officer was going to *ask* the individual politely to have a seat on the curb, stay in their vehicle, or whatever the case may be. If the person refused, the officer would *tell* them to do it by utilizing a strong command presence and a firm tone. If they still refused, then some type of control hold or takedown might be employed. As far as I was concerned, I was a "make me" kind of guy when it came to God. I was so stubborn - I didn't heed the little hints. God had to get my attention acutely, strongly, poignantly and traumatically. This part we'll call *the breakdown.*

I learned an important lesson about how God allows us to be torn down only to rebuild us with a better outlook so that we may become more spiritually mature. In my case, God had to allow me to break in order to get my full attention as I was so concerned with living in the world and what people thought of me. He removes all of the dark places of our old selves only to replace them with his light. He does this to use us for the greatness of His glory and to further His kingdom here on earth and in heaven. We cannot do this if we are spiritually dead. It made so much sense to me. God uses these "breaking" experiences to embolden us to carry out the work He has planned for us to do.

After we are broken is when we truly become more humble, less selfish and more teachable. Prior to being broken, you couldn't teach me anything because I already thought I knew everything. I was a tough nut to crack, and God allowed me to become broken under extreme circumstances in order for me to be humbled. Do you see the reasoning behind it? Although still a child of God, our Holy Creator had to break me down to my "right size," which was about the size of a peanut at that point. In retrospect, I can now see how God had to use this breaking experience of utter despair to finally shed my shroud of "greatness" and "self-sufficiency" in order to allow the Holy Spirit to start speaking and ministering to me.

This breaking point has caused me to realize several key points:

"For it is by grace you have been saved, through faith— and this is not from yourselves, it is the gift of God— not by works so that no one can boast" (Ephesians 2:8-9, NIV). God has saved me through the *blood* and *grace* of what Jesus Christ did on the cross for you and for me. I have been living in His grace and the knowledge of His salvation for several decades. But there was no spiritual growth on my part. I was stagnant; my attitude was like – well, I've got my free pass (salvation), and now I don't have to do anything else because I'm a believer. The Christian life requires more out of us as believers. I was still very much existing in the world and not living the Christian life as I should.

You see, after the salvation part comes *sanctification*. To be sanctified simply means to be set apart from or declared holy. Although we all live in this earthly world, we are set apart from it as believers. *"May God himself, the God of peace, sanctify you through and through. May your whole spirit, soul and body be kept blameless at the coming of our Lord Jesus Christ."* (1 Thessalonians 5:23, NIV). When we are sanctified, it simply means that we are no longer living in this world but rather growing in the knowledge of the Holy Trinity and allowing the Holy Spirit to minister and speak to us. Yes, our physical bodies are here on earth, but our minds are connected with our higher power, our Lord and our father. For a while, I used to see bumper stickers that stated, "NOW," which was an acronym for Not of This World. It makes perfect sense to me these days, but I didn't quite get it until I had a spiritual awakening.

After we receive our salvation as a believer and the sanctification process begins it is important to understand that sanctification is an ongoing process – it's like learning new skills throughout life; you just don't stop this spiritual growth until our earthly life comes to an end. Sanctification is what happens when the Holy Spirit is in the course of counseling and guiding us. When the Holy Spirit creates faith in us, he renews in us the likeness of God so that through His power, we may carry out God's will. We are "strengthened with power through His Spirit in our inner being" (Ephesians 3:16, NIV) so that we might live as those who are saved, sanctified, and serving. When our spiritual condition starts lacking or suffering in any way, a big red flag should go up. First, it's important to recognize when it happens. After we recognize it, we acknowledge it and uplift it in prayer.

The third key point is that once we are saved by His grace through faith and are sanctified, God wants us to be serving Him in some capacity. So, *service* is the watchword here. By serving mankind/womankind, we are, in turn, serving God himself. You may ask yourself, "Do I need to go to some faraway place or become a pastor at some megachurch in order to serve God?" The short answer is no, with the caveat that if that is what God calls you to do, then you must do it.

Your service could be a monumental undertaking, such as being a stay-at-home mom and raising your children in the ways of the Lord – being a great role model of what it means to love and serve. You may become an usher at church or drive the elderly to their doctor appointments. You'll know when the Holy Spirit calls you to something bigger because you'll feel Him tugging at your heart. Being of service to others gets us out of ourselves and focuses our thinking and inner-being on God and our fellow human beings. I find it to be a key ingredient in my sobriety and my spiritual connection with God.

Even when we are deeply conscious of our own great weakness when God calls us to do something, we draw encouragement from this: God is "able to do immeasurably more than all we ask or imagine, according to His power that is at work within us" (Ephesians 3:16, 20, NIV). God can get you through because He is God, and we are not. He has the power, mercy, and grace upon which to draw– even on the toughest of days and circumstances. In turn, as saved, sanctified servants of the Lord, we can pass His help, mercy, and grace to someone else who can really use it.

We grow in grace as the Spirit leads us. We take delight in the things that are not of this world and that are true, beautiful, and good. We rejoice in the small things and gain more serenity. That is not to say there won't be challenges and times of trouble. But we become better equipped to handle these trials as we grow in the Spirit and learn to rely on God for strength and wisdom. Our relationships with people get better as God changes our temperaments. You start realizing that God is working in your life as you start to feel his holy presence.

When we permit our past to crush us, in effect, we're telling God His grace isn't enough. Our Father extends His complete forgiveness to us regardless of what we've done. If we seek God's will, He will give us the grace to become the people we always should have been. God creates no mistakes. But rather, we squander what God has given us by imposing our own free will into everything we do instead of being led by the Spirit.

In Acts 9, God directed Ananias to heal Saul, a known persecutor of the church whom God had blinded. Ananias was incredulous at receiving this mission, stating that Saul had been rounding up believers in Jesus for persecution and even execution. God told Ananias not to focus on who Saul had been but on who he had become: an evangelist who would bring the good news to all of the known world, including the gentiles (those who weren't Jews) and to kings (v. 15). Ananias saw Saul the Pharisee and persecutor, but God saw Paul the apostle and evangelist. God had created a new and beautiful work in Saul, who had changed his name to Paul. After his transformation, Paul wrote, "Let us then approach God's throne of grace with confidence, so that we may receive mercy and find grace to help us in our time of need" (Hebrews 4:16).

We can sometimes view ourselves only as we have been—with all of our failures and shortcomings. But God sees us as new creations when we fully submit to Him, not who we were but who we are in Jesus and who we're becoming through the power of the Holy Spirit. He also does amazing work in each of our personal lives: giving us hope in the midst of suffering, giving us the Holy Spirit to understand His Word, and providing for our daily needs.

I am only scratching the surface as of the time of this writing. There is surely more room to explore and talk about deeper spirituality and God's promises. But I am still growing more spiritually every day and want to get the word of hope out there for anyone else who has struggled or is struggling with similar experiences as me. We take baby steps towards a better life, but sometimes people take bold and giant leaps. Everything happens for a reason if we become teachable and willing to learn about the nature of God and His amazing grace.

God is and was always there watching and loving me. He is never absent, but rather it was me who had not shown him the daily reverence and love that He deserves. God is always in our midst, forever omnipresent. It's just His nature. I only cared about my selfish needs and desires. I really needed to teach myself to see Him clearer in times of hopelessness and to see Him above all of my own doubts and human understanding. I finally had to let go and allow Him to work on His promises, even though I didn't understand the whole process. The beauty of it is that I don't have to understand it but just trust in the Lord. In doing so, I ask God for His will to be done and not my own. God's will for us is perfect, and He certainly knows what is better for me than I do. When I start imposing and inserting my own self-will, things start to go bad. That's why trusting in God every minute of every day gives me so much peace and serenity in my life.

The Lord has restored my life and my relationships. During my recovery, Lily has stood by my side and has been a true champion of God's love. I am blessed to have such a partner in life. I have made amends to everyone I had hurt. If they do not accept my deepest, sincere apology or are unwilling to forgive, that is on them and is something they will have to live with. I did my part and admitted my mistakes and sins against them. I am free of the bondage of alcohol and living in sin. Am I going to make mistakes? Of course, I am. That's what makes us human. But at least I don't have to wake up in the morning and apologize for something I had said or done the previous night. Life has become full of joy and serenity in just a short amount of time. With other people, it may take them longer to reach such a point as everyone's spiritual journey, and circumstances are different. The only thing another drink would get me is more time in jail, a divorce, or a metal pull-out bed inside of a morgue.

Amid the storms of life, Scripture points us to the safest place: "God is our refuge and strength, an ever-present help in trouble. Therefore we will not fear, though the earth may give way" (Psalm 46:1–2, NIV). Troubles will come; it's an inevitable fact of life. However, God outlasts them all. Those who run to the Savior discover that He can't be shaken. In the arms of His eternal love, we find our place of peace and solace.

Chapter 18

On Post-Traumatic Stress

During my 30-year career in law enforcement, there were terrifying moments when I thought I might not make it home at the end of my shift. Those shoot-don't shoot scenarios you see on television aren't that simple in real life. It is chilling to the core when you see your own life flash before your very eyes. It's not something you can easily dismiss or forget about. I remember every incident I was involved in that resulted in imminent death, and it'll always be back in the dark corners of my mind. I remember the homicides, the dead children, and the grieving family members I came in contact with. I shall never forget performing CPR on an infant in the passenger seat of a patrol car while another officer drove us quickly to the hospital in an attempt to save the child. That baby died in my arms. I remember driving up on a van where an estranged boyfriend had just stabbed his girlfriend to death multiple times. I'll never forget finding the lifeless body of an eight-year-old boy who had been shot in the back by a 14-year-old gang member. I've been on murder-suicide calls, and these are all things you can't un-see. Those events will always be with you forever, even into retirement. But the good news is that they do not have to haunt you forever.

When police officers confront the evils and darkness in the world on a routine basis, it begins to affect us unless we have a close connection and relationship with God. Contrary to what the media portrays of law enforcers today, we are humans, not robots. We have families and loved ones. We feel; we bleed; we care; we eat; we sleep, make mistakes, and go to work every day just like anyone else does. The only difference is that we do the things in society that nobody else has the courage or is willing to do. People get their ideas about law enforcement and policing from what they watch on television. Police officers may develop the feeling that they have the weight of the world on their shoulders because no one else understands them or what they do on a daily basis. Unfortunately, that is when the "us against them" mentality can set in if you allow it. We who have made an entire career in law enforcement are all survivors, but <u>we do not have to be victims</u>.

I learned that I AM NOT SPECIAL or UNIQUE. When we feel like we're walking through the fire, we feel all alone – like we're the only one with invisible wounds and is suffering in silence. In my journey towards resiliency, I have met so many wonderful people who have been through similar experiences and felt the same way. They, too, have found recovery and resilience by getting help and working on a holistic wellness program. We are human beings, and some suffer more than others.

Two divorces, being fired, officer-involved shootings, horrific scenes of carnage, a close friend dying in my home, the death of family members and friends, and dealing with death and other highly stressful situations in my profession had an adverse effect on my mental health. I succumbed to sadness, grief, stress, and darkness without properly seeking help. The vivid and recurring thoughts I had of some of those events became unwelcomed intruders that began to consume my life. Some people never come out of it, and others will die a sad and lonely death because of these events. I am living proof that there is a solution.

I have not disclosed every horrible thing I experienced in my life and career in this writing because that would require more writing time and paper. The point is that if these things aren't processed and dealt with properly, one can start on a downward hill towards self-destruction. Holding all of these things inside like a steel trap is not healthy. I learned that you have to talk about these things with someone; a friend, a close coworker, a pastor, or a counselor. However, I would not recommend talking to a spouse or significant other about these things as they can cause difficulties in the relationship. The important thing is to process these critical incidents and not suppress or tuck them away somewhere until you implode.

It is important first to recognize the symptoms of PTS before they are allowed to fester and cause problems in everyday life. Some of the common symptoms are nightmares, insomnia, recurring memories, loss of interest in things you once enjoyed, and hypervigilance. Some officers will experience a sense of "superhero" syndrome on the job in which they will take unnecessary risks because they do not care about what happens to them. Other officers will clam up on the job and will fail to perform their job duties out of fear. I experienced almost all of these symptoms at different times.

The longer you've worked as a first responder will undoubtedly expose you to more traumatic events. It's kind of like an analogy of a bucket in which we start our careers with a clean slate, and the bucket is empty. The more water that is added to the bucket, the more unstable the bucket becomes. One day several more drops of water are added to the bucket, and the bucket is pushed over the limit and spills over. That's what sometimes happens to people. We may be very effective at our jobs, and we effectively deal with and solve crises on a daily basis. But it's how we process these events after the fact that is critical to our good mental health.

With more information that is being made available, law enforcement agencies are getting better at dealing with post-traumatic stress. The last agency I worked for now conducts critical incident stress debriefings with a licensed mental health professional after every officer-involved shooting. But it wasn't always that way. When I started in law enforcement, there was a stereotype that police officers were these macho, physically fit knuckle draggers who just kicked butt and handled calls. They were expected to suck it up and digest the bad stuff without paying attention to how they felt or their mental health. Anything less was a sign of weakness. Thank the good Lord those days are slowly going by the wayside.

Eventually, I began to deal with my alcohol problem in a healthy manner. Then I tried to overcome my issues with PTS. I tried hypnotherapy, talk therapy and took over-the-counter supplements that were supposed to help with alcohol cessation and stress. However, none of this stuff worked. What did work for me was something called Eye Movement Desensitization and Reprocessing (EMDR) therapy. I went to a licensed psychologist in Prescott, Arizona, who was also trained and certified to provide EMDR therapy. The process is not easy for me to explain, but the therapist guided me through the process of reliving several traumatic events that I had dwelled on. Although I relived these incidents during the therapy session, it was in a controlled and safe environment. My brain was able to reprocess my trauma, and I felt like a weight had been lifted off of my shoulders when I was done. This may not work for everyone, but this type of therapy is widely utilized at Veterans Administration hospitals with great results.

I would like to discuss *secondary trauma* briefly. It is also known as *empathy fatigue* and is the type of PTS that comes from helping people, i.e., victims of crimes, survivors of violence, surviving family members of deceased victims, etc. It's the type of stress that comes from helping people day in and day out or witnessing or helping a person go through something awful. The stress and hardship of what you're experiencing, seeing, and feeling eventually take a toll on you. If you are an empath like me, chances are you may bring the victim's grief or trauma home with you after your shift is over. I've heard people say things like, "Oh, just leave work at work;" or, "When I get off shift, I leave the uniform at work." That's all fine and dandy, but we all have brains, minds, and memories. We bring those memories home with us at the end of the day, and sometimes we do not process or handle it well. As empathetic individuals, we tend to take on a victim's grief.

Chapter 19

The Four Pillars of Resilience

If you've spent time in law enforcement, you would know that experiencing trauma on the job is part of an unwritten understanding and an unpleasant component of the profession. After all, we are witness to mass casualty events, child death, officer-involved shootings, horrific car wrecks, violence, and other forms of human misery. So, who wouldn't be affected by these types of incidents to one degree or another?

I personally struggled with issues related to post-traumatic stress and began to self-medicate with alcohol to numb the emotional pain I was experiencing. Unfortunately, it wasn't just one or two incidents that slowly caused me to meltdown but the cumulative effects of experiencing significant dynamic events over a 30-year career in police work. Research reveals that it is not a single incident in many cases but rather a culmination of continued exposure to these events that can lead an officer down a crooked path to self-destructive behavior. Unless proper intervention and healthy lifestyle changes are sought, this unhealthy conduct can lead to adverse and even catastrophic outcomes.

Some officers may be the type of individuals who are *one and done*. In other words, they may experience their first and only officer-involved shooting, and they completely melt down. I know people like that. Sadly, one of them committed suicide, and the others got out of the law enforcement profession altogether. It does not mean they are weak, but quite the opposite. They recognized they did not want to continue in such a profession and that their psyche and body couldn't handle such trauma. Most of the officers I know who quit police work sought help and eventually went on to live healthy, productive, and fulfilling lives.

I recently had a conversation with someone I consider a friend. We speak frequently and have a deep mutual respect for each other. When talking about the on-duty shooting he had in 2001, he said, "I got in a shooting and lost my mind." I thought about his statement for a moment and related to the part about losing one's mind because I've also felt that way in the past. Then I replied, "No, you got in a shooting and experienced post-traumatic stress. Your mind and psyche were hurt, but you didn't lose your mind." He was one of the guys who decided that he'd get out of law enforcement after working in the profession for eight years. He's doing well today and can openly talk about his experiences with PTS. That's what emotionally healthy and resilient people do. They get help, reinvent themselves, and press forward.

So, let's discuss the organizational culture in the law enforcement profession for a moment. When I got into law enforcement in 1985, we didn't talk about trauma because it was viewed as a sign of weakness. We may have joked about horrific things we were involved in with our peers because that was a cynical way of letting out the stress and misery we witnessed. It was a way of expressing our emotional pain without the appearance of being weak and indisposed. After all, I was unwilling to give up the "coolness and strength" image that I felt I projected on the job.

The term *post-traumatic stress* wasn't even around in the 80s, so we just shook off the mental injuries of the day and went about our business. Reporting to your superior that you may have issues with post-traumatic stress is not a popular or comfortable position. Losing face or possibly being reassigned to administrative duties pending a professional diagnosis is absolutely terrifying. Thus, the negative stigma of self-reporting such human frailty is allowed to fester in the profession. There is a significant problem with post-traumatic stress in the first responder professions (police, fire, medical, EMS), and it needs to change. The organizational culture is slowly getting better, but more attention needs to be focused on this very critical area.

Recent studies have found that over 35% of police have indicated experiencing some form of post-traumatic stress compared to 6.8% of the general population (Heyman et al., 2018). Several studies have even shown officers experiencing post-traumatic stress to be more than 40%. Many law enforcement officers have died by their hands due to experiencing post-traumatic stress and depression, which could have been prevented by implementing healthy lifestyle changes and coping strategies. Other peripheral contributing factors can exacerbate an officer's declining mental and physical state. Fatigue, poor diet, lack of sleep/shiftwork, job burnout, lack of support from management, and dysfunctional human relationships combined with post-traumatic stress is a powder keg just waiting to explode. The absence of positive interactions with the community can also lay a toxic foundation for overall officer wellness.

Prevention and daily maintenance are the keys to career survival and personal resilience.

Unfortunately, 2019 also brought a surge in police suicides in the United States, provoking heightened media attention that leads administrators and experts to consider the possibility of contagion within the more significant mental health issues facing the law enforcement profession. In addition, small groups of suicides within single agencies, such as the New York City Police Department (NYPD), have contributed to an almost frantic response by administrators and experts to try and find a solution. Regrettably, there has been insufficient research on the causes of police suicide. Nevertheless, psychology has developed evidence-based responses that can be turned to search for practical and meaningful applications for law enforcement.

The military has also successfully implemented various resiliency training approaches that are slowly catching on in the law enforcement community. However, although the military culture and organization have apparent similarities to policing, such interventions still need to be rigorously tested by law enforcement (Chopko and Schwartz, 2013).

It should also be stressed that officers are more likely to receive assistance immediately following critical incidents. This phenomenon is because the long-term effects of both primary and secondary trauma can manifest suddenly or after a significant period of time.

As previously mentioned, the military has developed and instituted resiliency training for its service members. More specifically, the U.S. Air Force (USAF) and the Defense Logistics Agency (DLA) have advanced, improved, and revised their concept of the *Four Pillars of Resilience* (or well-being), which includes the mental, physical, social, and spiritual components of our lives with much success. These *four pillars* help to bring balance into our lives and work in congruency with each other. When one neglects one of the pillars or areas of their life, it affects the other three pillars.

By strengthening these four pillars, we become more resilient. Instead of experiencing an overwhelming downward spiral when we encounter stress in our lives, these four pillars work together to lift us up out of the mental chaos we are feeling. I discovered these pillars and implemented them in my own life as a holistic approach to wellness and abstinence from alcoholic beverages and other mental health therapeutic techniques.

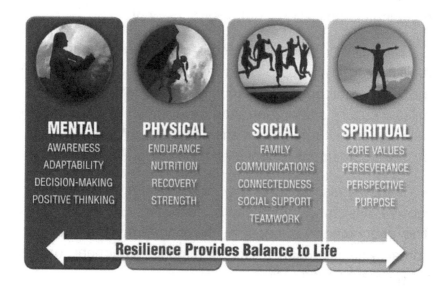

MENTAL	PHYSICAL	SOCIAL	SPIRITUAL
AWARENESS	ENDURANCE	FAMILY	CORE VALUES
ADAPTABILITY	NUTRITION	COMMUNICATIONS	PERSEVERANCE
DECISION-MAKING	RECOVERY	CONNECTEDNESS	PERSPECTIVE
POSITIVE THINKING	STRENGTH	SOCIAL SUPPORT	PURPOSE
		TEAMWORK	

Resilience Provides Balance to Life

The *Four Pillars* work in conjunction with each other to bring balance to our lives.

Mental Pillar

The mental pillar has to do with one's ability to cope with mental stressors and challenges effectively. As we begin to master working on the mental pillar, we start paying more attention to our needs and feelings. Remember, our thoughts control our energy. The mental pillar is about working on your mental state of mind or psychological resilience. Getting the right amount of sleep is vital in maintaining mental strength and building resilience. It's no secret that getting enough sleep is essential to our physical and mental functioning in everyday life. Sufficient sleep can help with on-the-spot decision-making and reaction time. An adequate amount of sleep is said to be seven to nine hours or more if you perform high-stress physical and mental activities.

Building Resilience Through Mental Toughness

Mental Toughness refers to the ability to stay strong in the face of adversity; to keep your focus and determination despite the difficulties you encounter. A mentally tough individual sees challenge and adversity as an opportunity and not a threat and has the confidence and positive approach to take what comes in their stride (Strycharczyk, 2015).

According to Strycharczyk and Cloughe (n.d.), techniques for developing mental toughness revolve around five themes:

1. Positive Thinking
2. Anxiety Control
3. Visualization
4. Goal Setting
5. Attentional Control

Generally speaking, mentally tough individuals appear to achieve more than the mentally sensitive and enjoy greater contentment. Positive thinking impacts what is known, felt, and believed to be true. Positive self-talk can help to overcome negative thoughts. Also, having an attitude of gratitude for the things in life one is thankful for can significantly help lower stress levels while removing negative thoughts.

Visualization, an internal focus on positive mental images, can impact both mind and body favorably. Mental rehearsal is a proven way to prepare for challenges and to assert control over your psyche. Picturing positive outcomes in one's mind can help condition one's mind to successfully achieve positive outcomes.

Attentional control increases your capacity to focus. Concentrating on the right thing, especially under pressure, can be learned through setting goals, removing distractions, and using routines to embed knowledge better.

Finally, when it comes to goal setting, using clear, realistic, and achievable goals can focus and energize you and provide long-lasting motivation.

Further Strategies from
The American Psychological Association

Make Connections - Resilience can be strengthened through our connection to family, friends, and community. Healthy relationships with people who care about you and will listen to your problems, offer support during difficult times, and can help us to reclaim hope. Likewise, assisting others in their time of need can benefit us greatly and foster our sense of resilience.

Avoid seeing crises as insurmountable problems - We cannot change the external events happening around us, but we can control our reaction to these events. There will always be challenges in life, but it's important to look beyond whatever stressful situation you are faced with and remember that circumstances will change. Take notice of the subtle ways in which you may already start feeling better as you deal with the difficult situation.

Accept that change is a part of living - They say that the only thing constant in life is change. As a result of difficult circumstances, specific goals may no longer be realistic or attainable. Accepting that which you cannot change allows you to focus on the things you do have control over.

Move toward your goals - Though it is important to develop long-term, big-picture goals, it is essential to make sure they're realistic. Creating small, actionable steps makes our goals achievable and helps us to regularly work towards these goals, creating small "wins" along the way. Try to accomplish one small step towards your goal every day.

Take decisive actions - Instead of shying away from problems and stresses, wishing they would just go away, try to take decisive action whenever possible.

Look for opportunities for self-discovery - Sometimes, tragedy can result in great learnings and personal growth. Living through a challenging situation can increase our self-confidence and sense of self-worth, strengthen our relationships, and teach us a great deal about ourselves. Many people who have experienced hardship have also reported a heightened appreciation for life and deepened spirituality.

Nurture a positive view of yourself - Working to develop confidence in yourself can be beneficial in preventing difficulties and building resilience. Having a positive view of yourself is crucial for problem-solving and trusting your own instincts.

Keep things in proper perspective - When times get tough, always remember that things could be worse; try to avoid blowing things out of proportion. Cultivating resilience helps to keep a long-term perspective when facing difficult or painful events.

Maintain a hopeful outlook - When we focus on what is negative about a situation and remain in a fearful state, we are less likely to find a solution. Therefore, try to maintain a hopeful, optimistic outlook, and expect a positive outcome instead of a negative one. Again, visualization can be a helpful technique in this respect.

Take care of yourself - Self-care is an essential strategy for building resilience and helps to keep your mind and body healthy enough to deal with difficult situations as they arise. Taking care of yourself means paying attention to your own needs and feelings and engaging in activities that bring you joy and relaxation. Regular physical exercise is also a great form of self-care.

Physical Pillar

Physical wellness means avoiding substance abuse, eating a balanced diet, and incorporating regular exercise into your daily routines, all of which will keep your body running better and longer.

It's kind of a *no-brainer*. We all know that working out is good for us. But as stated earlier, the physical pillar works in congruency with the three other pillars to help bring balance to life. The following are common benefits associated with working out or exerting physical activity:

a) Improves your memory and brain function (all age groups).
b) Protects against many chronic diseases.
c) Aids in weight management.
d) Lowers blood pressure and improves heart health.
e) Improves your quality of sleep.
    i) Good sleep enhances mental focus, clarity, and memory.
    ii) Good sleep enhances the immune system.
    iii)   Good sleep = better mood.
    iv)   Good sleep can increase and improve physical performance.
    v)   Good sleep can help reduce the effects of stress.

f) Reduces feelings of anxiety and depression.
g) Combats cancer-related fatigue.
h) Improves joint pain and stiffness.
i) i. Maintains muscle strength and balance.
j) j. Increases life span.

Now that we've examined the Mental and Spiritual Pillars, let's look at the remaining two areas that contribute to building resilience.

Social Pillar

Everyone needs a *wingman* or *battle buddy*. First-responders often refer to their unit or coworkers as a "second family" to who they can turn for support, friendship, and even protection. For this reason, public safety members need to pursue social wellness, find friendship and support in both their professional and personal lives, to feel a sense of belonging, and cultivate respect for others.

Social Wellness means using good communication skills and actively seeking opportunities to connect with others in a personal way:

Good communication skills are an important part of understanding others and being understood. Socially well individuals are respectful and authentic with others, generously sharing their thoughts, stories, and feelings and noticing when it's better to listen than to speak.

Seeking opportunities to connect with others means maintaining and creating relationships and indicates ease and comfort in social situations. Whether through social networking sites, social gatherings among friends and family, or over the phone, socially well individuals are active participants in their relationships.

Social wellness means developing healthy attachments and knowing how to cope with unhealthy relationships:

Developing healthy relationships instead of unhealthy attachments is a significant differentiation when discussing social wellness. Healthy relationships are characterized by mutual respect, equal give and take, and the overall positive influence the attachment has on the lives of those involved in the relationship. In addition, healthy relationships can provide us with good feedback, affirmation, and purpose.

Coping with unhealthy relationships can be just as important as maintaining good relationships. Socially well individuals can recognize when a relationship is harmful to them and can part from negative relationships. In other words, we cut toxic people out of our lives whenever possible.

Lastly, a healthy respect for others assists in forming authentic relationships based on openness, trust, and understanding. Socially well individuals treat all connections courteously and openly. They do not pass judgment on others based on race, sex, religion, or ethnicity but instead choose to explore diversity in their social interactions.

Spiritual Pillar

The *spiritual pillar* seems to be the area most neglected in our lives. People forget that we are mental, physical, social, and *spiritual* beings. It is important to remember all four components when it comes to resilience.

Spirituality is expressed in many forms, whether tied to a religion, a moral philosophy, or an inherent sense of connectedness with something greater than oneself. In any form, spirituality is always personal. The need for spiritual wellness is often downplayed as less important than emotional, physical, or social health but is vital to the overall wellness of every human being. The Spiritual Pillar is not necessarily about being tied to a religion, but it can be. It is a personal choice and is very relevant to our resilience.

For me, personally, it is very easy to apply to my own life. I was raised in a Christian home as a child and have believed in a Judeo-Christian God for as long as I can remember. These early formed beliefs have helped form a fundamental spiritual basis in my life. However, I teach on this topic in a public university and do not impose my personal religious beliefs on the students. Therefore, this is the part of the book where I secularize spirituality or keep it nonsectarian.

Spiritual Wellness means making time to contemplate your purpose in life and achieving greater mindfulness of your impact on the rest of the world. Contemplating your purpose in life helps put you in touch with your potential to create, affect change, and increase good things in the world — like love, compassion, and peace.

Achieving greater mindfulness is necessary in order to locate yourself as a member of a global community. No man is an island, which means every person has significance and importance to others, including family members, friends, peers, neighbors, and beyond. Spiritually well individuals sense their implicit connection to others within their sphere of influence and outside it.

Spiritual wellness means having personal values and beliefs and acting compassionately in accordance with those values. Personal values and beliefs may change throughout the course of a lifetime, taking shape through the influence of relationships, events, and personal experiences. A spiritually healthy individual will take care to notice when their values shift, when to readjust them, and when to reassert their importance.

Acting compassionately is the physical expression of spiritual intention. Examples of compassionate action include prayer, efforts to find understanding in the midst of conflict, mentoring a peer, expressing love and affection, and other acts that cultivate mutual respect and nurture unity.

Signs of Spiritual Distress

- Loss of direction
- Sense of emptiness/feeling alone in the world
- Hopelessness and helplessness
- Withdrawal from family and friends
- Self-destructive language
- Bitter or jaded outlook on life
- Fearfulness, dissociation (identity disorder)
- Anger at God/higher power

An attitude of caring for others can really help connect us with our spiritual side. I heard the following quote in a class I took many years ago. It is an ancient philosophy but is still very applicable today:

"Regard your soldiers as your children, and they will follow you into the deepest valleys; look upon them as your own beloved sons, and they will stand by you even unto death."

~ Sun Tzu

It is my desire that you adopt these four pillars into your own lives and see how positive change can improve your overall outlook over time.

Conclusion

Alcohol and drug abuse (legal and illicit drugs) almost always go hand in hand with PTS. Just go to the domiciliary at any veteran's hospital, and you will witness the tragedy of PTS combined with substance abuse. It does take a lot of courage to seek help. It is uncomfortable and can be embarrassing, but if you think you may have a problem or similar issues, you will thank yourself in the long run if you get help now. The cunning and baffling thing about alcohol is that it is like the Big Bad Wolf and is always standing ready at the front door, just waiting to destroy your house. The first drink almost always leads to more which can certainly escort us down a pathway to sorrow and destruction. Some people can drink normally and responsibly. However, I am not one of them and have crossed over into that problem drinker category – an alcoholic.

I never woke up one day and said, "I have a great idea; I think I'll become an alcoholic!" I doubt no alcoholic has ever done so. I was a pretty normal kid from a healthy, loving family. I started out as a social drinker. I used to get "happy" or would become silly when I first started drinking. The longer time and greater quantity I drank, I became a belligerent, angry drunk. My behavior almost caused me to lose my relationship with my wife and children after retiring. This is the tragedy of alcoholism as it is a progressive disease. It becomes like an old friend and a comfort to some people. Then it sneaks up and takes your soul if you allow it.

Drinking was a byproduct of my PTS. There could always be a debate about whether a person was already predisposed to alcoholism, or was the out-of-control drinking directly caused by PTS? I honestly do not know the answer to that question. I know that alcoholism is now considered a primary disease and that medical and mental health professionals recognize that fact. I can say that my PTS was interfering with my ability to live my life healthily and functionally for me. First, I made a wrong choice by turning to "the drink" for some relief. Then I became more and more dependent on it, switching from wine to hard liquor. If I was predisposed to being an alcoholic, my abnormal drinking habits were undoubtedly exacerbated by my PTS. It's a vicious circle and chain reaction. Alcoholism is non-discriminatory as it can affect anyone.

For me, it takes a loving, trusting, and daily relationship with God and being an active participant in the program of Alcoholics Anonymous. I am not endorsing AA, but I am simply saying that's what I need for myself in order to live a full and healthy life. I feel very comfortable and at ease with my fellow AA meeting attendees, some of which are current or retired medical doctors, firefighters, police officers, and military folks. I tried hypnotherapy, talk therapy, and some supplements for alcohol cessation. None of it worked. What works for me may not work for everyone else. I need the Holy Trinity (God the Father, Son, and Holy Spirit) and to practice the principles of AA in my daily life so that I may continue to live life to its fullest. I am happy, joyous, and truly free when I do so. Being aware of the Four Pillars of Resilience and working on them daily helps add another layer of protection to my overall well-being. God has changed my character, personality, and outlook on everything for the better. I am no longer stressed out, angry, depressed, or short-tempered. I no longer feel consumed by the feeling that something bad will happen. Instead, I feel grateful most days and am thankful for the new life that I have received.

I have recounted all of the times when I should have been killed. Several of those incidents were mentioned in this book, but there were other times as well. Being run over by a pickup truck and not having a scratch, being shot at a handful of times and never being hit by the gunfire, and being in several car crashes and walking away are all true examples of miracles. I believe I was clearly saved through divine intervention and by the grace of God. I feel that God kept me alive for a reason; so that I can share His love and the Gospel of Jesus with others. None of us know the day or the hour of our death. But I will no longer squander whatever time I have left in this earthly life.

God is the maker and master of miracles. He has promised us in His Word, *"...because of your partnership in the gospel from the first day until now, being confident of this, that he who began a good work in you will carry it on to completion until the day of Christ Jesus."* (Philippians 1:5-6, NIV). We've all heard the expression, "Let go and let God." It sounds so simple, sophomoric, and almost cliché. Yet, there is so much undeniable truth and power in that statement.

When we allow God to become the master, ruler, and loving father of our lives, we let go of the hurts of the past and receive God's peace and serenity. It's in God's word, "And the peace of God, which surpasses all understanding, will guard your hearts and your minds in Christ Jesus" (Philippians 4:7, ESV). Every component of my life has become enriched because I have taken a step back and allowed God to be my Lord, master, and king. I am in constant contact with God throughout each day. I find myself praying to Him when I drive, when I'm kayaking on a serene lake, or sitting quietly in my home. When I see something that requires God's intervention, like driving by the scene of a traffic accident or a homeless veteran standing on a street corner, I usually say a little prayer. Life isn't all about me, and when I think and feel about other people, it makes me feel something good inside.

We are all bound together through our humanity and that we were all created by the same god. That is quite a contrast from the old me, who was hardened and unable to break from the untrusting, cynical, hypervigilant, and judgmental mentality I used to have. How could I be bound together with my earthly brothers and sisters when I was "so much better" than so many of them! I can now sarcastically say that because I was so self-centered and egocentric before I fully surrendered to God. He could not use me for His good back then. After all, who was going to listen to such a worldly and misguided person? I first had to walk through the fire of life and become broken in order to step out into the light. Now, the bad experiences I went through can be used as a vessel for God's purposes. The same may also be true of you and your circumstances!

I connect with God daily through prayer, meditation, reflection, and studying scripture. I also read several different short devotionals, which give me encouragement and inspiration to draw closer to God each day. I find myself talking to God all of the time, like when I'm driving, waiting in a lobby to go into an appointment, and every morning when my feet hit the floor. I pray at bedtime and church every Sunday, which also keeps me in fellowship with other believers.

Not everyone is going to like or respect you. It's just part of the human factor and a fact of life. We all mess up, and some people are just very critical and unforgiving of others. Those people can work out their own character defects with God someday if they so choose to do. But we are not put on this earth to be liked by a multitude of people. If I focus my mind and life's activities on the Lord, I do not have to be concerned about being liked or offending people the way I did in my drinking days. However, there is the only one we should strive to please, and that is our Almighty God. The more we try to emulate the nature of God, the better we become. We will never be holy, as Jesus is and was the only truly holy man when he walked this earth over 2000 years ago.

I'm trying to make a point to be true to yourself and stay close to your maker. Nobody is perfect, but we should all shoot for spiritual growth as our daily goal. If you surrender to the Lord, you will be amazed at the amount of grace that will be present in your life. Take it from me, who was once a pessimistic naysayer, and now I fully believe in God's power. I have seen it, felt it, and experienced the magnificence of God in my life. I am speaking my truth, and some people may not like it. I say seek what is beautiful, good, compassionate, right, and holy to them.

Although there has been some recent controversy about who wrote the Serenity Prayer, the words of the prayer resonate as a solid and true reminder that we cannot change the past.

"God, grant me the serenity to accept the things I cannot change,
Courage to change the things I can,
And wisdom to know the difference."

But if we accept what has happened and ask God for the courage to change the things we can, He will be faithful to help us along the way. Having the wisdom to know the difference is just simply knowing that what has been done is done. There is no undoing the past. However, we can change for the better if we have the desire and turn our will and lives over to God's care. We can make a conscious decision today to fully surrender to the Lord God and to allow Him to lead us through the trials of life.

This writing is an invitation and a call into action. I hope and pray that this book may inspire you in some small way. If you are hurting or feel like there is no way out of this life other than by means of self-destruction, please reach out and talk to someone who can take your hand and lead you on the road to healing, the pathway to Christ. I shall leave you with this blessing, *"Now may the Lord of peace himself give you peace at all times and in every way. The Lord be with all of you."* (2 Thessalonians 3:16, NIV).

~The End~

Amanda, Lily, Keith, and Alexandra ("Alix") Knotek

Bibliography

American Psychological Association (n.d.). Retrieved from
   https://www.apa.org/topics/resilience

Chopko, B. A., & Schwartz, R. C. (2013). The relation
   between mindfulness and posttraumatic stress
   symptoms among police officers. *Journal of Loss and
   Trauma, 18*(1), 1–9.
   https://doi.org/10.1080/15325024.2012.674442

Clough P, Strycharczyk D (2015) Developing mental
   toughness. Kogan Page, London

Heyman M., Dill J., Douglas R. (2018). The Ruderman White
   Paper on Mental Health and First Responders.
   Retrieved from
   https://issuu.com/rudermanfoundation/docs/first_respon
   der_white_paper_final_ac270d530f8bfb

Military One Source (n.d.) Retrieved from
   https://www.militaryonesource.mil/national-
   guard/psychological-health-program/spiritual-
   wellness/#:~:text=Spiritual%20wellness%20means%20
   having%20personal,relationships%2C%20events%20a
   nd%20personal%20experiences.

About the Author

Keith Knotek is a retired sheriff's sergeant and police commander with thirty years of law enforcement experience in California. He also wrote several books, including his latest book, *Gunrunner*, which he co-authored with Mario Oliveira. The first edition of From Sorrow to Amazing Grace: One Cop's Journey was turned into a movie titled One Cop's Journey. Keith has been featured on television, radio, and podcasts and currently speaks at conferences, events, and training seminars discussing wellness.

Keith is a graduate of the FBI Law Enforcement Executive Development Association Regional Command College, California POST Executive Course, California POST Sherman Block Supervisory Institute, and holds an MA in Organizational Leadership and a BS in Criminal Justice. He is an adjunct university instructor and lectures on topics related to mental health, resilience, and law enforcement. Keith is an Advisory Board member for the Violently Injured Police Officers Organization (VIPO) and enjoys volunteering, boating, and fishing. He lives in Prescott, Arizona, with his wife, Lily, and has two adult daughters.

Made in USA - Kendallville, IN
42909_9781948278508
12.10.2023 1319